ROME

THE SECRET ATLAS

JONGLEZ PUBLISHING

THE AUTHORS

Ginevra Lovatelli organises original private tours to discover Rome. Website: secretrome.com

Adriano Morabito, a Rome native who is still passionate about his city and its less well-known sites, began focusing his attention on urban speleology in 1999. He is one of the founders of 'Roma Sotterranea', an association active in the exploration and study of underground tombs of historical and archaeological interest: roma-sotterranea.it

A Rome native who still lives in the Campo Marzio district, Marco Gradozzi has a passion for archaeology, photography, music and folk traditions. He has been an active participant in the 'Roma Sotterranea' association since 2005. Website: romasurvey.it

Nicole Cabassu was born and lives in Avignon, the 'other Rome'. A professor in classics, she is particularly interested in the literary and artistic approach to Roman cultural heritage.

Other contributors: Damiano Vergari, Hélène Vuillermet, Jacopo Barbarigo, Marylène Malbert, Ariane Varela Braga, Viviana Cortes and Ophilia Ramnhaut.

We have taken great pleasure in drawing up 'Rome – The secret atlas' and hope that through its guidance you will, like us, continue to discover unusual, hidden or little-known aspects of the city. Descriptions of certain places are accompanied by thematic sections highlighting historical details or anecdotes as an aid to understanding the city in all its complexity. 'Rome – The secret atlas' also draws attention to the multitude of details found in places that we may pass every day without noticing. These are an invitation to look more closely at the urban landscape and, more generally, a means of seeing our own city with the curiosity and attention that we often display while travelling elsewhere…

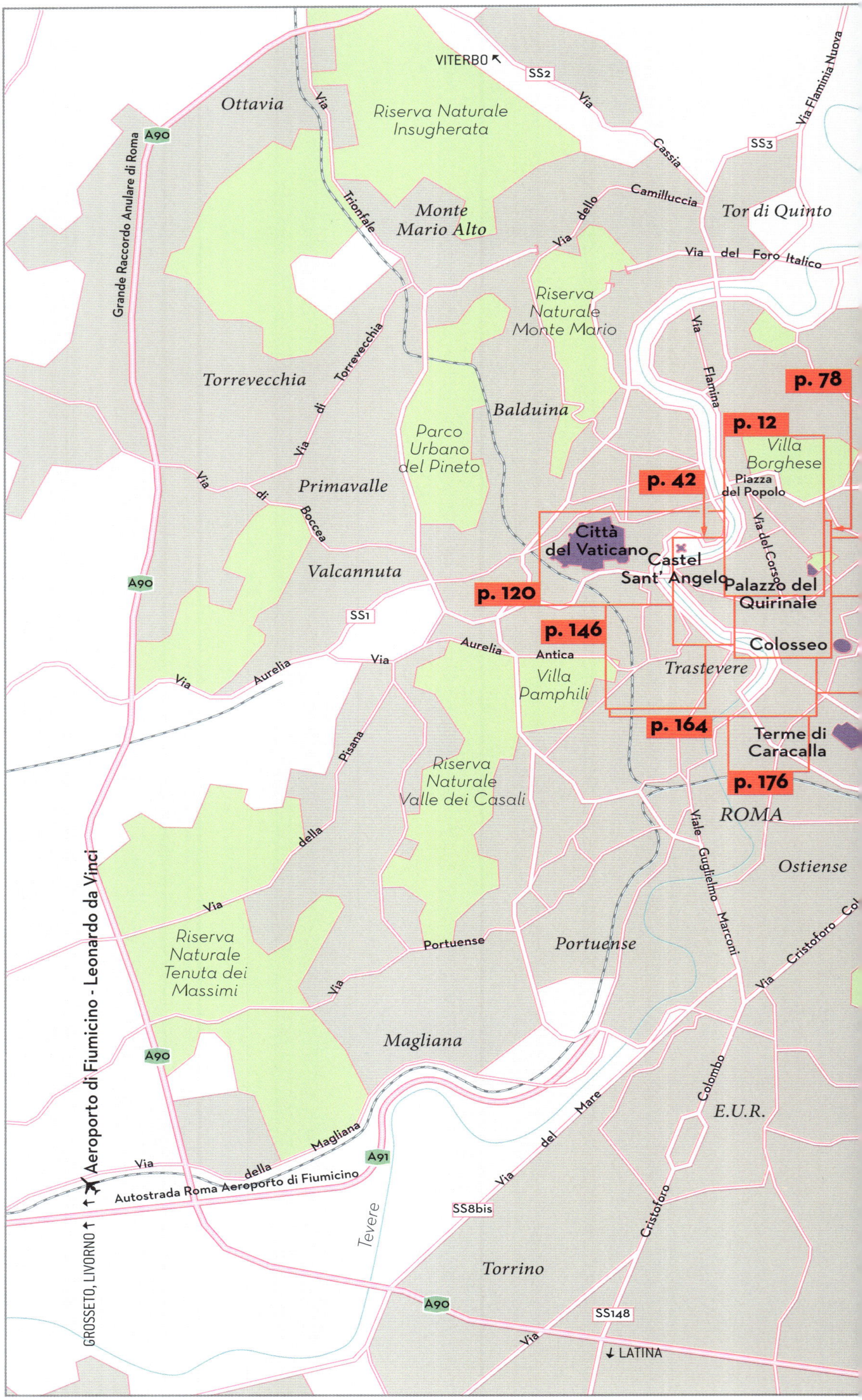

VITERBO
SS2
Via Cassia
Ottavia
Riserva Naturale Insugherata
A90
Grande Raccordo Anulare di Roma
SS3
Via Flaminia Nuova
Via Trionfale
Monte Mario Alto
Via della Camilluccia
Tor di Quinto
Via del Foro Italico
Riserva Naturale Monte Mario
Via Flaminia
Torrevecchia
Via di Torrevecchia
Balduina
Parco Urbano del Pineto
p. 78
p. 12
Villa Borghese
Piazza del Popolo
p. 42
Primavalle
Via di Boccea
Città del Vaticano
Castel Sant' Angelo
Via del Corso
Palazzo del Quirinale
Valcannuta
p. 120
SS1
p. 146
Colosseo
Via Aurelia
Via Aurelia Antica
Villa Pamphili
Trastevere
p. 164
Terme di Caracalla
p. 176
Via Pisana
Riserva Naturale Valle dei Casali
ROMA
Viale Guglielmo Marconi
Ostiense
Via della Pisana
Via Portuense
Portuense
Riserva Naturale Tenuta dei Massimi
Via Cristoforo Colombo
Magliana
Aeroporto di Fiumicino - Leonardo da Vinci
E.U.R.
Via del Mare
Via della Magliana
A91
Autostrada Roma Aeroporto di Fiumicino
SS8bis
Tevere
GROSSETO, LIVORNO
Torrino
A90
SS148
LATINA

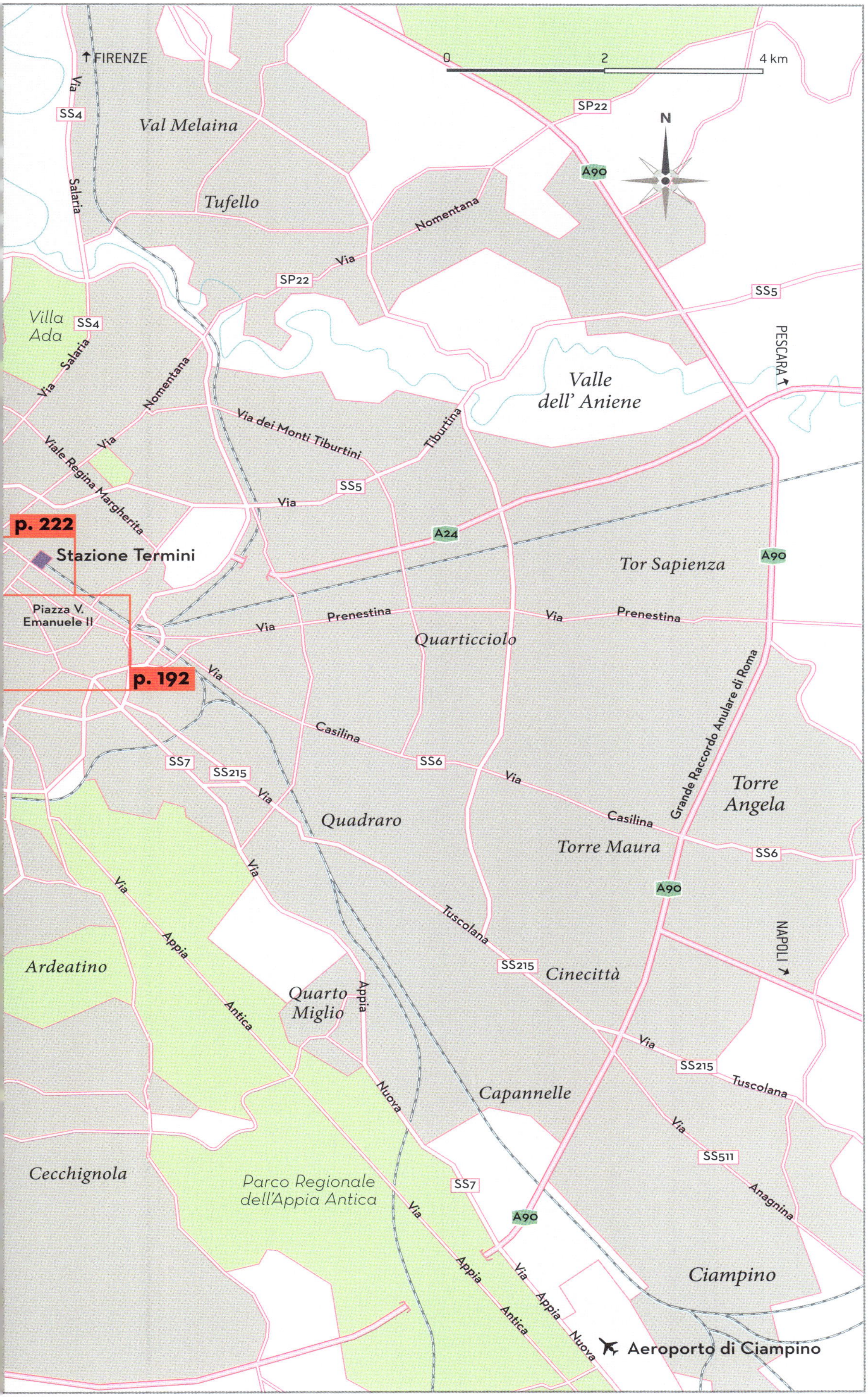

FIRENZE
0
2
4 km
N
Val Melaina
Tufello
Villa Ada
Via Salaria
SS4
SP22
A90
Via Nomentana
SS5
PESCARA
Valle dell' Aniene
Via dei Monti Tiburtini
Tiburtina
Viale Regina Margherita
p. 222
Stazione Termini
Piazza V. Emanuele II
p. 192
A24
Tor Sapienza
Via Prenestina
Quarticciolo
Via Casilina
SS6
Grande Raccordo Anulare di Roma
Torre Angela
Torre Maura
SS7
SS215
Quadraro
Via Tuscolana
Cinecittà
NAPOLI
Ardeatino
Quarto Miglio
Via Appia Antica
Via Appia Nuova
Capannelle
SS511
Via Anagnina
Cecchignola
Parco Regionale dell'Appia Antica
Ciampino
Aeroporto di Ciampino

CENTRE NORTH

CENTRE WEST

CENTRE SOUTH

THE VATICAN AND SURROUNDING AREA

GIANICOLO

TRASTEVERE

AVENTINO - TESTACCIO

LATRAN – COLOSSEUM – FORUM – CELIO

QUIRINALE – TERMINI – MONTI – ESQUILINO

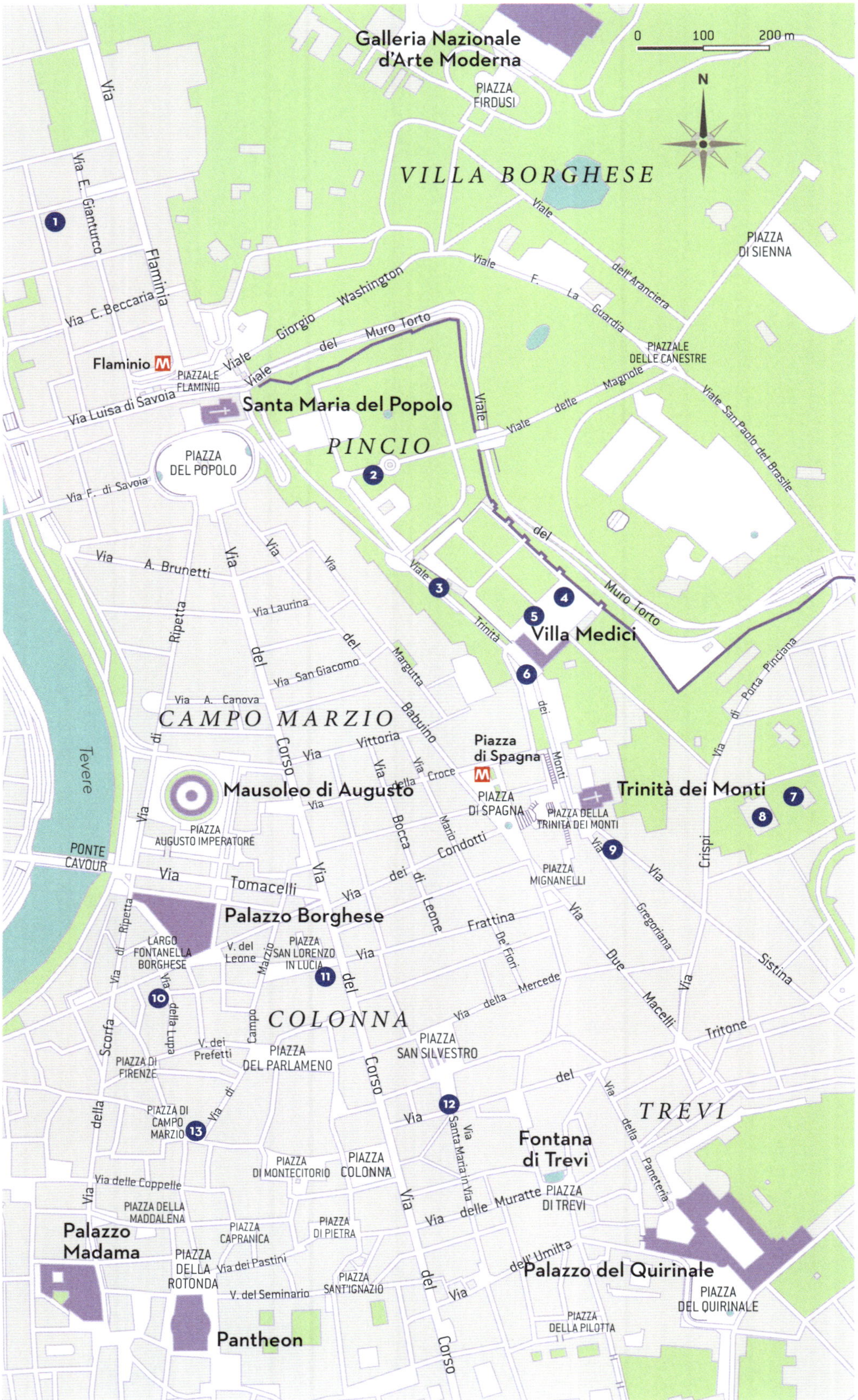
Galleria Nazionale d'Arte Moderna
PIAZZA FIRDUSI
0 100 200 m
N
VILLA BORGHESE
PIAZZA DI SIENNA
Viale F. La Guardia
Viale dell'Aranciera
Viale Giorgio Washington
Viale del Muro Torto
PIAZZALE DELLE CANESTRE
Viale delle Magnolie
Viale San Paolo del Brasile
Flaminio
PIAZZALE FLAMINIO
Via Flaminia
Via E. Gianturco
Via C. Beccaria
Via Luisa di Savoia
Santa Maria del Popolo
PINCIO
PIAZZA DEL POPOLO
Via F. di Savoia
Via A. Brunetti
Via Laurina
Via San Giacomo
Viale Trinità
Villa Medici
Via di Porta Pinciana
Via di Ripetta
Via A. Canova
CAMPO MARZIO
Via del Corso
Via del Babuino
Via Margutta
Via Vittoria
Via della Croce
Piazza di Spagna
Via dei Monti
Trinità dei Monti
PIAZZA DI SPAGNA
PIAZZA DELLA TRINITÀ DEI MONTI
Tevere
Mausoleo di Augusto
PIAZZA AUGUSTO IMPERATORE
PONTE CAVOUR
Via Tomacelli
Via Bocca di Leone
Via Mario de' Fiori
Via Condotti
Via Crispi
Via Sistina
Via Gregoriana
PIAZZA MIGNANELLI
Via Frattina
Via Due Macelli
Palazzo Borghese
LARGO FONTANELLA BORGHESE
V. del Leone
PIAZZA SAN LORENZO IN LUCINA
Via Campo Marzio
Via della Scrofa
Via della Lupa
Via della Mercede
Via del Tritone
COLONNA
V. dei Prefetti
PIAZZA DI FIRENZE
PIAZZA DEL PARLAMENO
PIAZZA SAN SILVESTRO
TREVI
PIAZZA DI CAMPO MARZIO
Via Santa Maria in Via
Fontana di Trevi
Via della Panetteria
PIAZZA DI MONTECITORIO
PIAZZA COLONNA
Via delle Coppelle
PIAZZA DELLA MADDALENA
Via delle Muratte
PIAZZA DI TREVI
Palazzo Madama
PIAZZA CAPRANICA
PIAZZA DI PIETRA
PIAZZA DELLA ROTONDA
Via dei Pastini
Via dell'Umiltà
Palazzo del Quirinale
V. del Seminario
PIAZZA SANT'IGNAZIO
PIAZZA DEL QUIRINALE
PIAZZA DELLA PILOTTA
Pantheon
1
2
3
4
5
6
7
8
9
10
11
12
13

CENTRE NORTH

01.

Villa Helene
Via Pasquale Stanislao Mancini, 20
Tram 2, 19 or Metro A – Flaminio

HENDRIK CHRISTIAN ANDERSEN MUSEUM

The artist's residence as a museum

Villa Helene is an elegant building just a stone's throw from the Tiber. It was built in 1922 by the Norwegian sculptor and painter Hendrik Christian Andersen, who moved to Rome in 1897. The villa is an extremely interesting example of a studio-residence transformed into a museum, and it was reopened to the public after restoration work in 1999. The ground floor is composed of the studio, where Andersen planned and created his works, which he then exhibited to the public in the other room, the gallery. There are about forty large plaster and bronze sculptures exhibited in both areas. The first floor, once the artist's residence, has drawings, paintings and smaller sculptures.

Over 200 sculptures, as many paintings and about three hundred pieces of graphic art, including drawings and plans, make up a collection that is not only surprising in terms of its size, but also and especially because everything, except the paintings, is dedicated to the artist's sole great plan, the creation of a 'world city'. To disseminate his idea of a utopian modern city that would be an experimental centre of new ideas for art, philosophy, religion and science, Andersen and the architect Ernest Hebrard published an illustrated book in 1913 entitled *Creation of a World Centre of Communication*.

A visit in the spring is particularly pleasant as you can sit and enjoy a drink in the *Caffè del Museo* and take a break in the sun on the lovely first-floor terrace.

02.

Pincio
Metro A – Spagna; Bus 117

THE BUST OF FATHER SECCHI

A testimony to the meridian crossing Rome

Not far from Casina Valadier, among the 223 sculptures of famous people scattered across Pincian Hill, a bust stands out.
The small pillar on which the sculpture sits is pierced with a hole and bears the inscription *Meridiano dell'Osservatorio del Collegio Romano*.
Looking through the hole (which is actually a lens) towards the city, at a distance of 1.22 kilometres, the church of Saint Ignatius can be seen. Above it sits the remains of the observatory. It was here, in 1852, that 32-year-old Jesuit priest Father Secchi installed his Merz refractor telescope, equipped with a 24-centimetre aperture lens and a focal length of some 4.35 metres.
Father Secchi died in 1878. He dedicated his life not only to astronomy (he discovered double stars, nebulas and comets), but also to meteorology, geography, geodetic measurements, physics, chemistry and archaeology. On his death, the city paid tribute to him by inaugurating a bust in his memory.
Among countless other scientific activities, Father Secchi determined the longitude and latitude of his observatory and linked the Rome meridian to the prime meridians of the time.
Calculating the meridian was essential in determining the position of the stars and for astronomical timekeeping.
Its position needed to be extremely precise and regularly monitored. So to make sure his instrument was perfectly stable, in 1860 he designed a simple but ingenuous system: he placed on Pincian Hill a 'disc' comprised of alternating black and white quadrants, like the one that can be seen today on the pillar supporting his bust.
Originally, the target was placed on a tree, but to ensure the utmost precision, the Jesuit later had a column erected upon which a marble chessboard could be inserted via a small hole under the disc.

Nearby, within the north-west outer wall of the Villa Medici, lies another disc. Beside it can be read the date '1822' – a much earlier date than Father Secchi's scientific activities. This is where, in 1774, Pope Clement XIV founded the Collegio Romano Observatory.

MERIDIANO
DELL
OSSERVATORIO
DEL COLLEGIO
ROMANO

03.

The French Academy in Rome – Villa Medici
Viale della Trinità dei Monti, 1
Metro A – Spagna; Bus 119 – Trinità dei Monti

GALILEO'S COLUMN

The memory of Galileo, imprisoned at the Villa Medici

Near the western façade of the Villa Medici, few passers-by notice a curious column of black marble, barely distinguishable from the surrounding vegetation.
Installed by the city of Rome in 1887, it commemorates the stay of one of the villa's most illustrious guests: Galileo Galilei. Accused of heresy by the Roman Inquisition, the greatest scientist of his age found refuge at the villa on two occasions.
Under the protection of Cosimo II de' Medici, Grand Duke of Tuscany, who had appointed him 'extraordinary mathematician' at the University of Pisa, Galileo was free to pursue his research without interference. Grateful for this support, he honoured his patron by naming a constellation he observed for the first time in 1610 the 'Medicean Stars'.
Contrary to the Church's doctrine at the time, Galileo was a staunch advocate of heliocentric theories, which posited that the Earth revolves around the sun. Firmly convinced of the validity of the Copernican system, he faced severe criticism and was summoned to defend himself before the Congregation of the Holy Office in Rome. On this first occasion, Cosimo II, to whom Galileo appealed for leave, offered him hospitality by providing two rooms in the Villa Medici.
Full of hope, Galileo arrived in the papal city on 12 December 1615. However, the discussions were heated. Amid the fervour of the Counter-Reformation, the Roman Inquisition strongly condemned Copernicus' work. Ordered by the Grand Duke of Tuscany to return immediately to Florence, Galileo reluctantly left the Villa Medici on 4 June 1616.
After several years of relative quiet, hostility toward Galileo's research intensified. Summoned once more to stand trial before the Roman Inquisition in 1633, he faced a lengthy legal process that culminated in his being condemned to imprisonment on 22 June 1633. Thanks to the intervention of some Tuscan political allies, the Pope commuted Galileo's sentence, replacing imprisonment with enforced residence at the Villa Medici, to which he was escorted on 24 June. However, clemency was soon granted, and on 6 July 1633, Galileo departed the Villa Medici for the last time.

IL PROSSIMO PALAZZO
GIA DE MEDICI
PRIGIONE A GALILEO
REO D'AVER VEDUTO
TERRA VOLGERSI INTORNO AL
S.P.Q.R
MDCCCLXXXVII

04.

Villa Medici
Viale Trinità dei Monti, 1
Metro A – Spagna; Bus 119 – Trinità dei Monti

THE BAS-RELIEF DEPICTING THE JUDGEMENT OF PÂRIS

The Greek bas-relief that inspired Manet's *Déjeuner sur l'herbe*

On the far right of the façade looking into the garden of the Villa Medici is a 3rd-century Greek bas-relief representing the Judgement of Pâris. The relief was originally found on the front of a Roman sarcophagus that Raphael undoubtedly came across in Cardinal Andrea della Valle's courtyard of antiquities in 1510. Raphael's drawing has since been lost, but in 1515 it inspired an engraving by Marcantonio Raimondi (1480–1534) that was then widely distributed. It is said that Raimondi's engraving was the inspiration behind Manet's *Déjeuner sur l'herbe*.

Three characters can be seen in the lower right-hand corner of this bas-relief: a nymph sits naked among two river gods, one of whom is reclining, his lower body covered by a piece of cloth; the other, in the background, is only partly visible. The same composition can be found in Manet's painting, which caused a commotion when it was presented to the Salon des Refusés in 1863. It sparked controversy not only for its depiction of a naked woman sitting between two fully clothed men, but also because the woman's gaze is turned directly at the viewer.

The nymph in the original bas-relief is not turned towards the viewer. She does, however, face the viewer in Raimondi's engraving (in which the figure has a particularly androgynous quality). Manet's modern interpretation can be attributed to a reinterpretation of antiquity during the Renaissance.

The bas-relief is at the heart of an intricate web of inspirations and transformations. When it was bought by Ferdinando I de' Medici in 1584 and brought to the eponymous villa, an unknown artist added a personification of the zodiac in the sky to the top of the bas-relief on the front of the sarcophagus, as it appeared in Raimondi's engraving – Ferdinando's interest in astrology is well known.

This rare example of a work of art (a bas-relief) inspiring another work of art (an engraving), which in turn inspired the modification of the original work of art (the bas-relief) is what stands before us today.

A BAS-RELIEF THAT ALSO INSPIRED PICASSO?

Some have reported that the inspiration behind Picasso's *Demoiselles d'Avignon* could have come from the left side of the Greek bas-relief, which shows Paris awarding the apple to Venus; a daring assumption, even though Picasso reproduced the configuration of the right side, as did Manet, in several of his paintings.

05.

The French Academy in Rome – Villa Medici
Viale della Trinità dei Monti, 1
Metro A – Spagna; Bus 119 – Trinità dei Monti

THE ROMAN CISTERN AT VILLA MEDICI

A little-known witness to Rome's water supply

Visible only during temporary exhibitions at the villa or upon request, an ancient Roman cistern, hidden from street view, lies beneath the Villa Medici.

This immense reservoir, with a capacity of 1,300 cubic metres (now empty), is an extraordinary testament to the Pincian Hill's long-standing strategic role in supplying water to Rome.

As the site of one of the first major water-capture systems, the Pincian Hill became a crossroads for several ancient aqueducts, including the Aqua Virgo, which continues to deliver water to central Rome via a 19-kilometre-long tunnel. Benefiting from easy access to water thanks to these aqueducts, the hill became, from the 1st century BCE, an ideal location for large patrician villas adorned with gardens and fountains.

In 536 CE, during Emperor Justinian's campaign to reclaim Italy from the Ostrogoths, General Belisarius entered Rome and established his camp in the former palace of Emperor Honorius, the remains of which still lie buried beneath the Villa Medici. It was probably during this period that the Roman cistern was constructed, its vaulted roof supported by two massive pillars.

Although access to water became more challenging following the fall of the Roman Empire, the Renaissance marked a revival of ornamental gardens on the hill. In 1564, the land was purchased from the Crescenzi family and redeveloped by Cardinal Giovanni Ricci of Montepulciano, who commissioned the construction of what would become the Villa Medici. Appointed superintendent of waters, the cardinal also restored the Aqua Virgo aqueduct.

Surrounding himself with the finest engineers of the era, he tasked Camillo Agrippa with devising a system to supply fountains located tens of metres above ground, defying gravity, water was forced upwards using a pump powered by the motion of a water wheel.

After acquiring the villa in 1576, Ferdinand de' Medici, the future Grand Duke of Tuscany, continued his predecessor's transformations, enhancing the gardens with additional fountains.

© Assaf Shoshan

06.

Viale Trinità dei Monti, opposite Villa Medici
Metro A – Spagna; Bus 119 – Trinità dei Monti

THE CANNON BALL OF VIALE DELLA TRINITÀ DEI MONTI FOUNTAIN

A real cannon ball in the centre of a fountain

In line with the entrance to the Villa Medici is a majestic granite fountain that, with the panorama of Rome in the background, has inspired many artists, such as the painter Jean-Baptiste Camille Corot who immortalised the scene in 1826.

The basin of the fountain came from San Salvatore in Lauro; Cardinal Ferdinando de' Medici is thought to have acquired it from the monastery in 1587 for 200 ecus. The setting, however, came from a square close to San Pietro in Vincoli. It was probably constructed around 1589 by Annibale Lippi, one of the architects of the Villa Medici.

There is an incredible story about the provenance of the cannon ball from which the water flows in the centre of the fountain.

In 1655, Queen Christina of Sweden, a prominent figure in 17th-century Roman life, is said to have had the cannon fired from Castel Sant'Angelo in the direction of the Villa Medici in an attempt to wake up the master of the house to go hunting. Three traces of the impact on the heavy door of the Villa bear out this version of events, while one of the balls was recovered to be set into the fountain opposite.

At the time, however, the villa was no longer much used by its then owner, Cardinal Carlo de' Medici.

Another theory goes that Queen Christina (a bit of a loose cannon herself) had promised the painter Charles Errard, director of the Académie de France in Rome, to knock at his door at a certain time of day. At the appointed hour, she was still at Castel Sant'Angelo and found a way of keeping her word by having the cannon pointed at the door of Villa Medici.

Note that this version is most certainly false: the Académie de France was established in 1666 with its headquarters at Sant'Onofrio (it only moved to the Villa Medici in 1803, having successively occupied several Roman palaces). What does seem sure, however, is that these legends grew up not only to justify the marks on the door, but also the impetuous character of Queen Christina of Sweden!

ACADEMIE NATIONALE DE FRANCE

07.

Via Ludovisi, 48
Metro A – Barberini; Bus 100 – Ludovisi/Emilia

VILLA MARAINI

A superb panoramic view from an artificial hill

In the heart of the Ludovisi district, close to Via Veneto, Villa Maraini offers one of the most spectacular views over the city: from the tower of the villa is a 360° panoramic viewpoint that is only 3 metres lower than the belvedere on the dome of Saint Peter's Basilica.
This luxurious and eclectic building combining Renaissance and Baroque influences was built between 1903 and 1905 by Emilio Maraini, a successful captain of industry born in Lugano, Switzerland, in 1853.
He began to produce sugar from beets that he had grown in the countryside around Rieti and in a few years became the 'sugar king'.
He then obtained Italian citizenship and even became a member of parliament, which is why he moved to Rome. A short distance from the church of Trinità dei Monti he bought some land where tonnes of stone, gravel and rubble had been piled up, partly for the construction of Via Ludovisi. Rather than just dispose of the rubbish, Maraini had the idea of building his house on top of this artificial hill.
The majestic three-storey villa, set in lush gardens, was designed by his architect brother Otto, who was also involved with the construction of the Excelsior Hotel on Via Veneto.
Inside, stucco, columns, frescoes, tapestries and marble figures grace the rooms, among which is the unmissable grand ballroom overlooking a loggia open to the garden. The monumental staircase with its three landings, flanked by two columns and graced with an incredible marble parapet, leading from the ground floor to the first floor, is very impressive.
The villa's decorations are the originals, embellished with copies of antique sculptures.
The owner's widow, Countess Carolina Maraini-Sommaruga, donated the villa to the Swiss Confederation in 1947. Since 1949, it has been home to the Swiss Institute, whose mission is to promote scientific and artistic exchanges between Switzerland and Italy.

08.

Capella da Sylva, church of Sant'Isidoro
Via degli Artisti, 41
Metro A – Barberini

THE BREASTS OF BERNINI'S 'CHARITY' AND 'TRUTH'

Sensuality censored

Some works of art can inflame the spirit more than others. If the nudes of Michelangelo's Last Judgment provoked such a scandal that Pope Paul IV had their private parts covered up (a delicate task entrusted to Daniele da Volterra, who has gone down in history as the '*braghettone*' or breeches maker), Bernini's sensual sculptures created for the Da Sylva chapel – although less well known – met a similar fate.

The chapel is in the church of Sant'Isidoro, near Piazza Barberini. Construction of the church for the Spanish Franciscan community began in 1622.

It was dedicated to Isidore of Madrid, patron saint of agriculture. A few years later the unfinished building was handed over to a group of Irish Franciscans. They had assembled in Rome around Brother Luca Wadding, who had founded a college with a well-stocked library there.

In 1663, the small Cappella da Sylva was added to the right of the high altar, to accommodate the funerary monuments of the family of Portuguese nobleman Rodrigo Lopez da Sylva, knight of the Order of Saint James and eminent member of the Iberian community in Rome.

On the left is a bas-relief monument to Rodrigo and his wife Beatriz da Silveira, framed by the naked figures of Charity, who seems to be offering her breast to visitors, and Truth, with a radiant sun on her breast, both sculptures by Giulio Cartari.

On the right is the monument to his son Francisco Nicolò da Silva and his wife Juana, flanked by representations of Justice and Peace, the work of Paolo Naldini.

All the bas-relief portraits were made at a later date, in the early 18th century. The wall paintings and the *Immaculate Conception* at the rear of the chapel are by Carlo Maratta.

In the second half of the 19th century, 'Charity' and 'Truth', with their generous, sensual breasts, were deemed indecent by the Irish priests, who covered up their Baroque nudity with heavy bronze 'bras' fixed to the marble and painted so that they seemed part of the original.

The statues, which were restored in 2002, have now recaptured all their former evocative power.

09.

Palazzo Zuccari
Via Gregoriana
Metro A – Spagna

THE FAÇADE OF PALAZZO ZUCCARI

Monsters on the façade

Palazzo Zuccari occupies an area comprising the last part of Via Sistina and that of Via Gregoriana, and its façade is probably the most curious and unusual in the city. The cornices of the main door and of the windows are all formed by gaping monsters' mouths.
Federico Zuccari, the famous Baroque artist, bought the land in 1590, struck by its wonderful location, and he built the house and studio for himself and his children, drawing inspiration for the palace's façade from the 'monstrous' style of the famous monsters of Bomarzo, close to Viterbo. This architectural whimsy was both criticised and admired, but in any case soon became the ideal house for artists in the area. Through the Accademia di San Luca, Zuccari left the dwelling to foreign artists, but his wishes were not respected and when the artist died, the building was passed on to another owner. The Queen of Poland lived there from 1702 and for decades the house was the centre of high society in the city. After several changes of ownership, Zuccari's wish finally came true and the building became an inn for foreign artists. Winckelmann and Reynolds stayed there, David and Nazareni painted famous works there, and it appears in Il Piacere (The Child of Pleasure) by Gabriele D'Annunzio. In 1900 Henrietta Hertz, the last owner, left her collection of paintings to the Italian state and the palazzo and its library to Germany, allowing for the creation of the famous Biblioteca Hertziana (Hertzian Library), specialised in art history and still open today to scholars with special letters of recommendation.
The building, which is closed to the public for restoration, is full of important works, such as the frescoes of Giulio Romano.
In the basement the ruins of the villa of Lucullus, from the end of the Roman Republic, were found.

© Valerio Ceva Grimaldi

10.

Church of the Madonna del Divino Amore in Campo Marzio
Vicolo del Divino Amore, 12
Metro A – Spagna; Bus 119 – Fontanella Borghese

BLESSING OF THE THROATS

Protect your throat from the rigours of winter!

Once a year, in the deep midwinter, an extraordinary blessing helps you protect your throat and get through the winter safely. On 3 February, the feast day of Saint Blaise, masses are held throughout the day at the church of the Madonna del Divino Amore in Campo Marzio. After each mass, the priest gives the blessing by holding two candles in the form of a cross and touching people on the throat with them, repeating: 'Through the intercession of Saint Blaise, bishop and martyr, may God deliver you from ailments of the throat and from every other evil, in the name of the Father, the Son and the Holy Ghost.' The source of this tradition is the life of the saint himself (see opposite).

INNUMERABLE RELICS OF SAINT BLAISE

Blaise is probably the Roman Catholic saint with the greatest number of 'official' relics. If all those who claim possession are to be believed, Saint Blaise would have had over a hundred arm relics. Although his body is said to be buried at Maratea, in southern Italy, another body lies at San Marcello in Rome. The church of Santi Biagio e Carlo ai Catinari (Biagio is Italian for Blaise) allegedly retains the saint's 'throat bone'.

WHY IS SAINT BLAISE INVOKED TO PROTECT THE THROAT?

Born in the 3rd century CE in Armenia, Blaise was elected Bishop of Sebaste.

When the Christians began to be persecuted under Diocletian, he retreated to a cave surrounded by wild beasts, where he carried out several miracles including saving a child who was choking on a fishbone stuck in his throat. Blaise laid his hands on the child and prayed that he and all those who asked in his name should be healed, thus saving the child's life. Shortly afterwards, at his command, a wolf gave back a pig that it had seized from a poor woman. She later killed the pig and brought him its head and feet, with a candle and some bread. He ate the meat and told her that whoever lit a candle in a church dedicated to him would reap the benefit.

These two incidents were the source of the tradition of blessing the throat with wax candles. Tortured with an iron comb or rake, Blaise was finally beheaded in 287 or 316, according to different sources.

+ BLA SIV.

11.

Church of San Lorenzo in Lucina
Via in Lucina, 16a
Metro A – Spagna

POUSSIN'S TOMB

'Men of genius often herald their end with a masterpiece: it is their soul taking flight'

Poussin's tomb, commissioned by the French writer Chateaubriand between 1828 and 1832, when he was ambassador to Rome, is a white marble structure with a niche containing a bust of the painter. Below the bust figures a relief representation of his famous painting, *The Arcadian Shepherds*.

Strangely sited between two of the church's side chapels (tombs are usually in the side chapels), the tomb was sculpted by Léon Vaudoyer, Paul Lemoyne and Louis Desprez, three pupils of the Villa Medici, the headquarters of the Académie de France since 1803. Below the bas-relief, a Latin epitaph reads: 'Hold back your pious tears, in this tomb Poussin lives / He has given his life without himself knowing how to die / He is quiet here but if you want to hear him speak / It is surprising how he lives and speaks in his paintings'.

Although much ink has been spilled over the phrase 'Et in Arcadia ego', the existence of this tomb is probably only a straightforward homage to an artistic genius. As Chateaubriand said in *La vie de Rancé*, 'Admirable tremor of time! Men of genius often herald their end with a masterpiece: it is their soul taking flight'.

To learn more about the phrase 'Et in Arcadia ego', *see the following double page spread.*

T IN ARCA
EGO

'ET IN ARCADIA EGO'

The phrase 'Et in Arcadia ego' was probably used for the first time in a painting by Guercino, *The Shepherds of Arcadia* (1618), commissioned by the Barberini family and now in the museum of the Galleria Nazionale d'Arte Antica of the Palazzo Corsini, opposite the Farnesina. The words are shown carved on a block of masonry, by way of comment on two shepherds leaning on their staffs contemplating a skull. The phrase next appeared in Poussin's first version (1628–1630) of a painting by the same name (now in the collection of the Duke of Devonshire at Chatsworth House in the UK), before gaining fame in the second version of the picture, probably painted around 1638 and now in the Louvre in Paris.

Note that another, lesser-known painting kept at the Brive museum (France), entitled *Paysage aux bergers d'Arcadie* (anon., late 18th century), also bears the famous phrase and that a marble bas-relief in the garden of the English property of Shugborough Hall also deals with the subject. The interpretation of these words carved in stone has been endlessly discussed.

If Goethe, Schiller and Nietzsche understood it to mean, 'I too have lived in Arcadia [and I have been happy there]', the most commonly accepted interpretation (due in part to art historian Erwin Panofsky) is 'And even in Arcadia there I am [death]'. In other words, even in an idyllic and paradisiacal place like Arcadia, death is waiting for us all one day; stay humble and try to discriminate between the essential and the pointless and futile.

Without going into all the more or less far-fetched interpretations, some have seen links between this phrase and the celebrated enigma of Rennes-le-Château, several aspects of which make reference to Poussin's paintings. In one of the coded manuscripts discovered at the site appear the names of Poussin and the Belgian painter Teniers; the inscription 'Et in Arcadia ego' was also said to have been found there. Finally, some commentators have noted that the tomb in Poussin's painting and the surrounding countryside apparently corresponded to a tomb that once actually existed at Arques, near Rennes-le-Château. In 1978, researcher Franck Marie, like Pierre Jarnac in 1985, concluded that there was really nothing special about this tomb and that it had been dug in 1903 by the owner of the property, Jean Galibert, who had buried his mother and grandmother there. Their remains were exhumed and reburied elsewhere, most likely in the village cemetery, when the property was sold to Louis Lawrence, an American from Connecticut who had immigrated to the region. The latter, in turn, buried his mother and grandmother in the empty grave and had a tombstone bearing the inscription 'Et in Arcadia ego' erected. Louis Lawrence's son, Adrien Bourrel, told Franck Marie and Pierre Jarnac that he had seen the tombstone erected in 1933, when he was a teenager. Nevertheless, a certain Pierre Plantard had the time to completely fabricate his 'priory of Sion' while he was in prison and claimed that the tomb at Les Pontils had served as a model for Poussin's painting.

This tomb was finally demolished in 1988 by the owner of the property, with the authorization of the local authorities, so as to stop the visitors who came from around the world in search of esoteric revelations in vain.

Thus, far from having any fabricated esoteric meaning, Poussin's painting and the phrase 'Et in Arcadia ego' simply mean that death awaits us all one day.

ARCADIA: A TASTE OF PARADISE?

Arcadia is a mountainous region of Greece's central and eastern Peloponnese. In antiquity it was considered a primitive and idyllic place where shepherds lived in harmony with nature. In this respect it symbolised a golden age echoed by numerous literary and artistic works like Virgil's *Bucolics*. The ancient region, rediscovered during the Renaissance and the 17th century, notably through Poussin's painting *The Arcadian Shepherds*, is traversed by the Alpheus River which is said to run underground to the sea and resurface in Sicily. As Alpheus was a sacred river-god, the mythological son of the Titan Oceanus and his sister Tethys, whose underground streams symbolised the hidden traditions of esoteric knowledge, some have wrongly established a link between Arcadia and esotericism. The name Arcadia comes from Arcas, itself from the ancient Greek arktos, meaning 'bear'. Arcas, king of Arcadia, was in Greek mythology the son of Zeus and the nymph Callisto. The legend goes that Callisto had offended the goddess Artemis who changed her into a bear during a hunt. Callisto, killed in the chase, was placed among the stars by Zeus and became the *Ursa Major* (Great Bear) constellation, while her son Arcas was transformed into *Ursa Minor* on his death.

12.

Church of Santa Maria in Via – Cappella della Madonna del Pozzo
Via del Mortaro, 24
Metro A – Barberini

MIRACULOUS WATERS OF THE MADONNA DEL POZZO

In Rome as in Lourdes

Rome, like Lourdes, has its miraculous sources. You can, for example, visit the church of Santa Maria in Via in the heart of the city, behind the Alberto Sordi Gallery (located between Palazzo Chigi and the Trevi Fountain), and enter the Madonna del Pozzo chapel just to the left of the entrance. This is where, in 1256, the miracle took place that gave the church its popular epithet, 'little Lourdes'.

A well in Cardinal Capocci's stables began to overflow so copiously that the entire place was flooded. A painting on stone of the Virgin Mary, probably from the depths of the cistern, was floating on the water. The cardinal rescued it and built a small shrine at the site. The miraculous image has been venerated ever since as Our Lady of the Well.

The legend goes that those who had drunk water from the source soon experienced a miraculous recovery.

The site attracted more pilgrims and the church was enlarged in the 16th century.

Even today, from behind the railings in the chapel, the faithful can drink water from the well or take away small quantities for the sick.

POZZO
DELLA
B.VERGINE
ANNO·A·PARTV·VIRGINIS
IN·HAC·AEDE·QVAE·ERAT·OLIM
MIRACVLVM·VNIVERSO·ORBI
NOCTE·ENIM·AQVA·PVTEI
ADEO·SE·EXTVLIT
VT·E·QVI·IN·EO·MANENTES
NOVITATE·REI·EXTERRIT
ET·CAVSA·DILIGENT
AQVAM·EX·ORE
IN·EO·QVE·LAPIDEM
BEATAE·VIRGINIS·MARIAE
SVPERNATARE
CVMQVE·ILLVM·EXTRAH
OMNIA·CARDINALI
QVI·STATIM·HVC
DEO·QVE·CONFISVS
LAPIDEM
CVNCTAQVE·PONTIF
QVI·RE·BENE·DISCVSSA
STABVLVM·COMMVTARE
ITAQ·POPVLO·ROM·PVBLICIS
IN·QVIBVS·VENERAB
IPSO·PONTIFICE·COMITA
IN·HOC·IPSO·LOCO·ET·PROPE
REPOSV
ET·ECCLESIAM
SANCTA·MAR
IN·HOC·AVTEM·PVTEO
ET·PRAESERTIM·DE·PETRA
IN·QVO·D·N·IESVS
DVM·MIRABILE·ILLVD
CVM·BEATA·PHOTINA
REPONI
CVM·AVTEM·IN·POTV·HVIVS
SANCTISS·VIRGINIS·GRATIA
IN·DIES·MAGIS·MAGISQVE
CONTINVAR

13.

Church Santa Maria in Campo Marzio
Piazza di Campo Marzio, 45/A
Metro A – Spagna or Barberini

MASS IN ARAMAIC AT SANTA MARIA CHURCH IN CAMPO MARZIO

Mass in the language of Jesus

Hidden away in one of the most frequented parts of the historic centre, Santa Maria in Campo Marzio is an Eastern Catholic church of the Syrian-Antiochene rite but obedient to Rome, in which mass is celebrated in Aramaic at 10.30 every Sunday morning. The often sparse congregation and the blend of three languages in which the mass is said (Aramaic, Arabic and Italian), together with the majestic architecture of the church, create an ambience especially propitious to contemplation. After the service, worshippers are commonly invited to take coffee with the Patriarch.

The church dates back to the 8th century, when nuns fleeing from Constantinople during the persecution arrived in Rome and founded a convent. It was then acquired by the Benedictine nuns and enlarged to the size it is today, becoming one of the most important convents in the city. The entrance from the street leads to a splendid courtyard with a distinctive tau cross shape, an oasis of peace within the bustling city centre. It was designed by De Rossi, who was also responsible for reconstructing the church at the end of the 17th century. At the end of the courtyard, a very beautiful cloister with a central fountain can be glimpsed through a glass door, as well as one side of the church of San Gregorio Nazianzeno with its delicate little Romanesque belfry. This part of the complex is not open to visitors, as it is managed by the Italian Chamber of Deputies, which has undertaken major restoration work. The convent had fallen into serious disrepair and was expropriated after 1870, since when it has been occupied by various public offices.

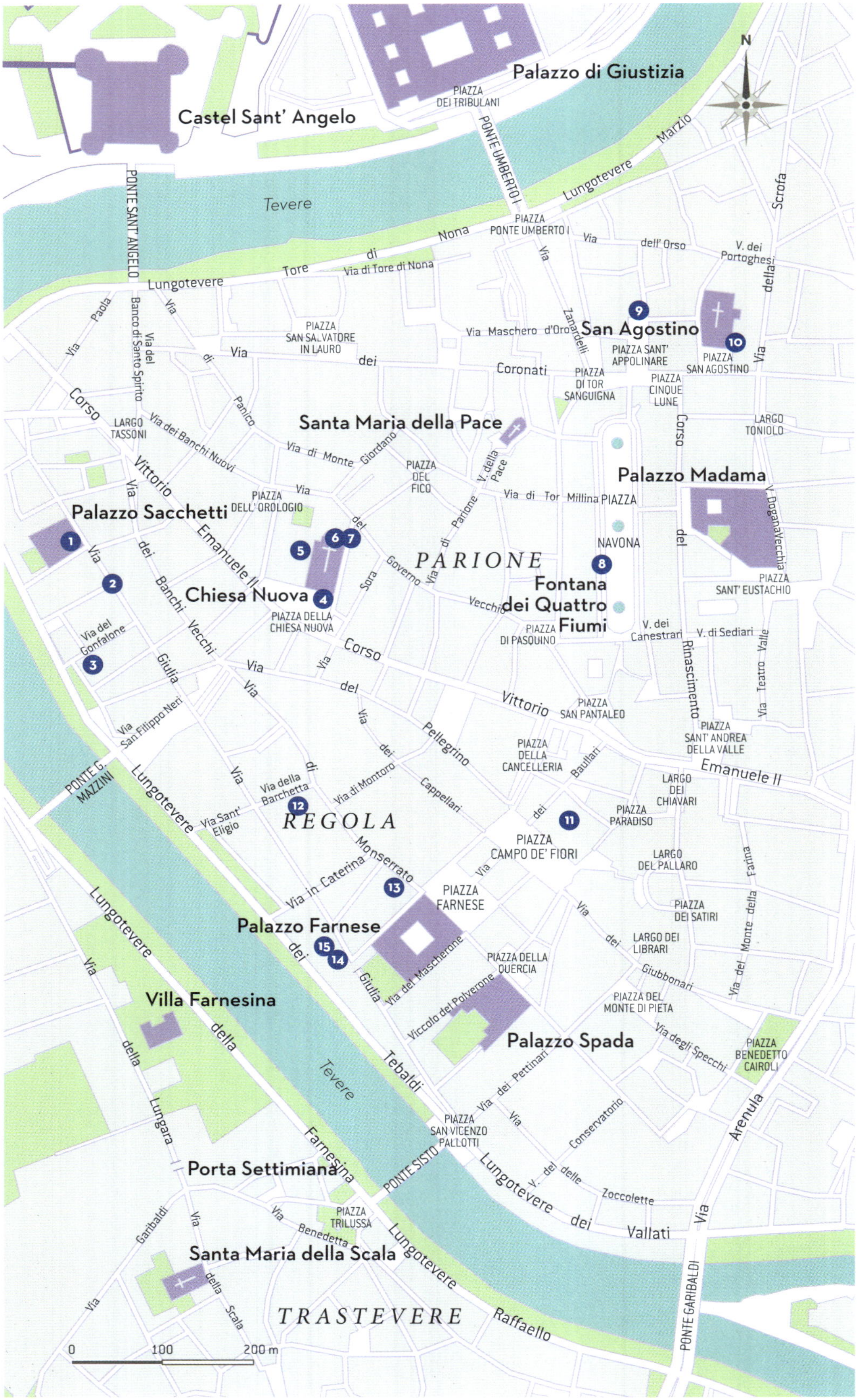

N
Castel Sant' Angelo
Palazzo di Giustizia
PIAZZA DEI TRIBULANI
PONTE UMBERTO I
PONTE SANT'ANGELO
Tevere
Lungotevere Marzio
PIAZZA PONTE UMBERTO I
Lungotevere Tor di Nona
Via di Tor di Nona
Via dell' Orso
V. dei Portoghesi
Via della Scrofa
Via Paola
Banco di Santo Spirito
Via del Banco di Santo Spirito
PIAZZA SAN SALVATORE IN LAURO
Via dei Coronati
Via Maschero d'Oro
Via Zanardelli
San Agostino
PIAZZA SANT' APPOLINARE
PIAZZA DI TOR SANGUIGNA
PIAZZA CINQUE LUNE
PIAZZA SAN AGOSTINO
Corso
LARGO TASSONI
Via dei Banchi Nuovi
Via Panico
Santa Maria della Pace
Via di Monte Giordano
PIAZZA DEL FICO
V. della Pace
LARGO TONIOLO
Palazzo Madama
Via di Tor Millina
PIAZZA NAVONA
V. Dogana Vecchia
Corso del Rinascimento
PIAZZA DELL' OROLOGIO
Palazzo Sacchetti
Corso Vittorio Emanuele II
Via dei Banchi Vecchi
Via del Governo Vecchio
Via di Parione
PARIONE
Fontana dei Quattro Fiumi
PIAZZA SANT' EUSTACHIO
Chiesa Nuova
PIAZZA DELLA CHIESA NUOVA
Via Sora
PIAZZA DI PASQUINO
V. dei Canestrari
V. di Sediari
Via Teatro Valle
Via del Gonfalone
Via Giulia
Via del Pellegrino
PIAZZA SAN PANTALEO
PIAZZA SANT' ANDREA DELLA VALLE
Via San Filippo Neri
PIAZZA DELLA CANCELLERIA
Via Baullari
PONTE G. MAZZINI
Lungotevere
Via della Barchetta
Via di Montoro
Via dei Cappellari
LARGO DEI CHIAVARI
Via Sant' Eligio
REGOLA
PIAZZA PARADISO
PIAZZA CAMPO DE' FIORI
Via di Monserrato
Via in Caterina
LARGO DEL PALLARO
PIAZZA FARNESE
Via Farina
PIAZZA DEI SATIRI
Palazzo Farnese
Via dei Giubbonari
LARGO DEI LIBRARI
Via del Monte della Farina
Lungotevere della Farnesina
Via dei Mascherone
PIAZZA DELLA QUERCIA
Villa Farnesina
Viccolo del Polverone
PIAZZA DEL MONTE DI PIETA
Via della Lungara
Palazzo Spada
Via degli Specchi
PIAZZA BENEDETTO CAIROLI
Tevere
Via dei Pettinari
Via del Conservatorio
Lungotevere dei Tebaldi
Via Arenula
PIAZZA SAN VICENZO PALLOTTI
PONTE SISTO
Porta Settimiana
V. delle Zoccolette
Lungotevere dei Vallati
Via Garibaldi
PIAZZA TRILUSSA
Via Benedetta
Santa Maria della Scala
Via della Scala
Lungotevere Raffaello
TRASTEVERE
PONTE GARIBALDI
0
100
200 m

CENTRE WEST

01.

Palazzo Sacchetti
Via Giulia, 66
Bus 62 – C.So Vittorio Emanuele/Tassoni

PRIVATE TOUR OF PALAZZO SACCHETTI

A jewel waiting to be discovered

The sumptuous Sacchetti Palace is still the residence of the family of that name, which explains why it is less famous than other Roman palaces, even though it was built and decorated by such renowned artists as Antonio da Sangallo and Francesco Salviati.
On the death of Sangallo, the original owner, the palace was bought by Cardinal Ricci di Montepulciano, who commissioned Nanni di Baccio Bigio to make some alterations, including the masterful Sala dei Mappamondi, with its walls frescoed by Salviati depicting scenes from the Old and New Testaments. The allegorical and mythological decorations of the majestic gallery were carried out by Giacomo Rocca.
In the middle of the 17th century, the palace passed into the hands of Cardinal Giulio Sacchetti, member of a family of Florentine merchants and bankers, who wasted no time in carving out a prominent position for himself in Roman society and acquiring the title of marquis, buying up vast properties in the Latium countryside and throwing himself enthusiastically into the business of artistic patronage.
Cardinal Giulio did not make many changes when he moved into this splendid palace, but he began to collect hundreds of precious objects, archaeological artefacts, and contemporary works of art, including some 20 paintings by Pietro da Cortona. Only two works remain from this remarkable collection, *Adam and Eve* and *The Holy Family*. The others have been dispersed, the fortunes of the Sacchetti family having sharply declined at the beginning of the 18th century following their dazzling rise up to the time of Cardinal Giulio, who at one point almost became pope.
At the side of the palace overlooking the Tiber, a recently restored nymphaeum still embellishes the garden, which used to run right down to the water before the construction of the quays. Within a small arcade are two niches with an ornamental basin and satyrs portrayed lifting a section of drapery to reveal an imaginary view of Rome. Above, the framed family coat of arms can be seen, surmounted by ephebes. In addition to the stucco, imitation marble, and mosaics, the artistic techniques used here are highly original: real shells embedded at various points alternate with festoons of fruit and flowers covered with coloured glass designs, not to mention the *tartari*, chalk formations imitating stalactites and stalagmites.

02.

Via Giulia,
from the junction of Via del Gonfalone as far as Vicolo del Cefalo
Bus 62 – C.So Vittorio Emanuele/Tassoni

THE 'SOFAS' ON VIA GIULIA

Remains of an aborted project

Only the base remains of the grandiose construction project for Palazzo dei Tribunali, designed by Bramante (see below). These huge blocks of travertine give an idea of the size of the building that was planned to bring together in one place the law courts of the papal government.

The stones are now incorporated into the walls of the buildings for some 100 metres, and project out into the street. As they vaguely resemble large cushions and give passers-by a chance to sit down, they soon came to be known as the 'sofas' on Via Giulia.

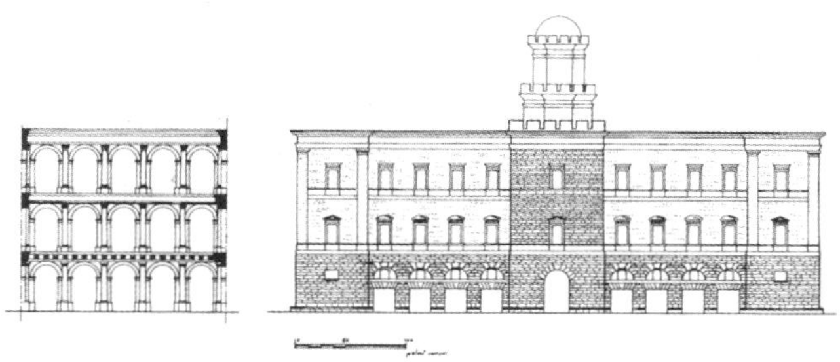

A FAILED PROJECT

Bramante and Pope Julius II della Rovere wished to make the new street the city's main artery. They planned it as long, straight, majestic and prestigious, according to the canons of the Renaissance – which it undoubtedly is. They also saw it as the heart of a new administrative district: the papal law courts were to be set up here and bourgeois residences would be built along the street. On this point their plans came to nothing. The courts never saw the light of day and the administration remained on the Campidoglio. Although some fine mansions were built, others were divided into rented apartments and small shops. A hundred and fifty years later, Pope Innocent X Pamphilj even had Rome's new prison built there (now, ironically, the anti-mafia headquarters), permanently laying to rest the monumental designs of his distant predecessor.

03.

Gonfalone oratory
Via del Gonfalone, 32/A
Bus 23 or 280 – Lungotevere Tebaldi/Perosi

GONFALONE ORATORY

A little-known marvel

This small marvel of the 16th century, hidden at the end of one of the many intersections of Via Giulia, once belonged to the important Archconfraternity of the Gonfalone. The oratory, which was restored between 1998 and 2002, remains almost unknown even though it is used today as a concert hall. It is, however, an extraordinary example of Roman Mannerism.

Although the building's small façade, by Domenico Castelli, is not particularly impressive, the interior is superb, with its walls completely covered with an extraordinary cycle of frescoes featuring the Passion of Christ in twelve parts.

They were painted in 1573 by Federico Zuccari, Livio Agresti, Cesare Nebbia, Bertoja, Raffaellino Da Reggio and Marco Pino. Wooden choir benches encircle the room. Also note the ceiling of carved and gilded wood, the work of Ambrogio Bonazzini dating from 1568.

Le Gonfalone means 'standard' or 'banner' and refers to the fact that, in the 14th century, Archconfraternity members used to raise the standard of the pope (who resided in Avignon at the time), as a sign of support for his sovereignty over Rome. The confraternity, whose members wore a white habit and blue hood, was also known for the organisation of processions and other religious ceremonies. Their representations of Christ's Passion were so realistic that the popes had to put a stop to them in order to prevent crowd violence towards the Jews. The Archconfraternity of the Gonfalone was dissolved at the end of the 19th century and the oratory fell into disuse, ending up in such a dilapidated state that it was used by refuse collectors as a storage area until a musician discovered this treasure and decided to use it as a concert hall.

04.

Piazza della Chiesa Nuova
Bus 64 – Chiesa Nuova

THE COVER OF THE 'TERRINA' FOUNTAIN

A fountain on the move

Designed by the architect Giacomo della Porta at the end of the 16th century, the fountain known to the ancient Romans as the 'Terrina' is today situated in the Piazza della Chiesa Nuova, opposite the Church of Santa Maria in Vallicella. The fountain attracts attention because of its curious shape, resembling a teapot. There is an interesting inscription, now almost completely worn away, carved around the border of the travertine cover: 'AMA DIO E NON FALLIRE FA DEL BENE E LASSA DIRE MDCXXII' (Love God, never fail to do good and let others say what they will, 1622). What appears at first sight to be a proverb was in fact a warning addressed to those who witnessed the executions (such as that of Giordano Bruno) that took place in the nearby Piazza Campo de' Fiori, the fountain's original location.
The spouts from which the water gushed were in the shape of a rose, probably because this flower appeared on the coat of arms of the Riario family, who owned the nearby Palace of the Chancellery (Palazzo della Cancelleria) (1485).
The edge of the marble basin used to be decorated with four bronze dolphins, made earlier for the famous fountain in the Piazza Mattei (also designed by Giacomo della Porta) but never used. (The upper basin of the Piazza Mattei fountain was left unadorned until 1658, when, following restoration work commissioned by Pope Alexander VII, the four famous turtles were placed there.)
In 1622, the bronze dolphins were dismantled and the fountain was covered with an enormous travertine lid, giving it the appearance of a tureen. The cover was probably installed to prevent the fountain's spouts from becoming clogged by waste from the market. When, in 1889, the monument to Giordano Bruno was erected in the centre of the Piazza Campo de' Fiori, the fountain was dismantled and placed in a city store until it was reinstalled, in 1924, on the Piazza della Chiesa Nuova.
A new fountain, similar to the 16th-century version, appeared on the west side of the Piazza Campo de' Fiori.

Unusually, the fountain sits below the level of the piazza. The architect decided to position it this way because the pressure of the Aqua Virgo Aqueduct was relatively low at this point.

05.

Piazza della Chiesa Nuova, 18
Bus 62 – C.So Vittorio Emanuele/Tassoni

MONUMENTAL HALL OF THE VALLICELLIANA LIBRARY

A saint's library

Few people are familiar with the majestic monumental hall of the Biblioteca Vallicelliana, which forms part of the Institute of the Oratory of Saint Philip Neri (the Oratorians are a congregation of secular priests), on crossing the threshold, it is difficult not to fall under the spell of this vast rectangular chamber, the true dimensions of which are invisible from the outside, illuminated as it is by sixteen overhanging windows.

Decorated with stucco, wood panelling, and the monochrome canvases of G.B. Romanelli, the ceiling is exceptionally luminous. Spiral staircases have been concealed in the four corners of the hall to avoid breaking the homogeneity of the book-covered walls. The splendid wooden bookshelves dating from the 17th century are divided into two levels by a gallery supported by columns. The earliest documents relating to the order, founded by the Florentine priest Filippo (Philip) Neri in 1565, date back to 1581, but the growing number of adherents and the need for space to store the ever-increasing donations required an extension. Francesco Borromini carried out this work from 1637 to 1652. Following the rules of their order, the Oratorians attach great importance to books; each meal, for example, is accompanied by a reading or commentary on a sacred text. The library, originally made up of the personal collection of the founding saint, has been constantly enriched over the years to arrive at the present total of some 130,000 volumes, including rare manuscripts, incunabula, illustrated books and musical scores. Most texts are concerned with history or theology, but philosophy, law, botany, astronomy, architecture and medicine are also represented, and there is an exceptional collection of engravings and photographs.

THE LIBRARY TRAPDOOR

Saint Philip Neri asserted that music was a 'fisher of souls' and the best form of spiritual diversion. Thus in the library there is a trapdoor that communicates with the oratory below, so that the music being played could be heard and inspire the readers above.

06.

Church of Santa Maria in Vallicella (Chiesa Nuova)
Piazza della Chiesa Nuova
Bus 40, 46, 62, 64 – Chiesa Nuova

THE SECRET ROOMS OF SAINT PHILIP NERI

Secrets of a saint unlike any other

Three times a week, if you pre-book, you can get into the so-called 'secret rooms of Saint Philip Neri'. Although the rooms are not the historical site where the saint lived and prayed, the visit is still of great interest thanks to the enthusiastic personality of Father Maurizio Botta, a Filippini (from Filippo, the Italian name of the order's founder) who shows all the visitors round. You will also discover some particularly impressive aspects of the life of this saint, who is little known to the general public.

The tour begins in the red room, where a number of saintly relics are displayed as well as an attractive outline of the saint's standard (17th century) which the faithful carried during the seven churches pilgrimage. In the reproduction of Saint Philip's chapel, you can see a lovely Guercino painting, *The Vision of Saint Philip Neri*.

Notable works on the upper floor include a fine fresco by Pietro da Cortona (*The Ecstasy of Saint Philip*) and a Guido Reni painting of *Saint Philip Contemplating the Virgin*.

WHY DOES THE FAÇADE OF THE ORATORY OF SAINT PHILIP NERI CURVE?

Borromini's façade for the Filippini convent (notably the home of the oratory) was designed to be in harmony with the adjoining church. Its curve is reminiscent of the human body, arms outstretched, as if to welcome all those who cross its threshold.

The façade of the church of Santa Maria in Vallicella is embellished with statues of Saint Gregory to the left and Saint Jerome to the right. They are associated respectively with Pope Gregory XIII, who gave the church to Saint Philip, and the convent of San Girolamo della Carità (see page 70) where he spent many years.

SPIRITUAL CONCERTS IN CHIESA NUOVA SACRISTY

Entrance at 3 Via di Chiesa Nuova

Once a month, from October to June, spiritual concerts in the revived tradition of Saint Philip Neri take place at 9pm in the superb sacristy of Chiesa Nuova.

SAINT PHILIP NERI: A SAINT WHOSE HEART DOUBLED IN SIZE AS HE RECEIVED THE HOLY SPIRIT

Founder of the Congregation of the Oratory, also known as the Congregation of Filippinis after his forename, Saint Philip Neri (1515–1595) was often referred to as the joyful saint because of his cheerful disposition.

Inspired by the early Christian communities, he wanted to anchor an intense spiritual life in daily routine based on prayer (he was one of the first to gather around him laymen with whom he prayed), reading, meditating on the word of God, and praising the Lord, mainly through chant and music.

According to him, music was a special way of reaching people's hearts and bringing them to God (see article on the trapdoor in the Vallicelliana Library for listening to music from the oratory below, page 52). Thus he became one of the most avid defenders of the rebirth of sacred music.

In 1544, while the saint was praying in the catacombs of Saint Sebastian over the tombs of the early martyrs, his heart was suddenly seized with immense joy and an intense light shone down on him. Raising his eyes, he saw a ball of fire which descended to his mouth and penetrated his chest. His heart, in contact with the flames, instantly dilated. The violence of the impact broke two of his ribs. The Holy Spirit had come to the saint, just as it had to the Apostles at Pentecost.

In the 17th century, a scientific autopsy on his body confirmed that his was twice the size of any other human heart. Nothing was the same again for Saint Philip. The beating of his heart was so strong that it could be heard some distance away and the heat that constantly devoured him meant he could face the rigours of winter in his shirtsleeves. The symbol of the congregation today, a heart in flames, is based on this episode of his life.

While looking after the sick, the poor and the infirm, he also took care to spend time with young people, wishing to stop them from falling into boredom and depression.

He often gathered a group around him and while always reminding them that life was to be lived joyfully, when the din became too loud one day, he is supposed to have said 'Quieten down a bit, my friends, if you can'!

His great spiritual gifts even enabled him to bring a child back to life for a few moments.

SAINT PHILIP NERI AND THE PILGRIMAGE TO THE SEVEN CHURCHES OF ROME

Bringing the early pilgrimages to Rome to the tombs of Saint Paul and Saint Peter back into fashion, Saint Philip Neri and his followers began to visit the principal centres of worship in the city. Over time, these informal visits grew into a veritable pilgrimage around the seven major churches of Rome: San Pietro in Vaticano, San Paolo fuori le mura, San Sebastiano fuori le mura, San Giovanni in Laterano, Santa Croce in Gerusalemme, San Lorenzo fuori le mura and Santa Maria Maggiore. Each journey represented one of the seven stages of Christ's Passion. The pilgrimage still takes place today – enquire at Chiesa Nuova.

07.

Church of Santa Maria in Vallicella (Chiesa Nuova)
Piazza della Chiesa Nuova
Bus 40, 46, 62, 64 – Chiesa Nuova

THE MOTORISED RUBENS

A painting that disappears once a week

Once a week, after the Saturday evening mass, Chiesa Nuova worshippers can take part in a very strange spectacle: the sexton lets down a Rubens painting by remote control to reveal a miraculous icon of the Virgin Mary behind it.

The source of this phenomenon dates back to the early 16th century.

At that time, a fresco depicting the Virgin and Child was on view outside, on the façade of a public bathhouse where the apse of the church now stands. In 1535, an unbeliever threw a stone at the image of the Virgin, who astonishingly began to bleed.

The image was placed inside the original Vallicella church for safekeeping. When the new church was built, following the installation of Saint Philip Neri's Congregation of the Oratory, the sacred image was in the first chapel to the right.

But the conditions for conservation of the fresco rapidly deteriorated and to safeguard it, the decision was made to place it behind the high altar. In 1606, Rubens was commissioned to paint a canvas that would serve to protect the image of the Virgin.

A first attempt failed, but in 1608 Rubens produced a work entitled *Angels Adoring the Madonna Vallicelliana*, which incorporated a special feature – a panel that could be removed to reveal, behind it, the miraculous holy image it was intended to protect.

08.

Brazilian Embassy
Piazza Navona, 14
Bus 30, 70, 81, 87 – Rinascimento

PALAZZO PAMPHILJ

The main gallery of the Brazilian Embassy

Palazzo Pamphilj, built in the 17th century, has accommodated the Brazilian Embassy since 1920. Twice a month, visitors who have booked ahead are shown round the seven magnificent chambers on the first floor (piano nobile), where biblical and mythological subjects alternate in the work of the most famous artists of the time: Giacinto Gimignani, Agostino Tassi (who went down in history as the rapist of Artemisia Gentileschi), Andrea Camassei, Gaspard Dughet and Giacinto Brandi.

The highlight of the visit is the main gallery, which is over 30 m wide and overlooks Piazza Navona. Designed by Francesco Borromini and decorated (1651–1654) by Pietro da Cortona, whose fresco cycle depicts scenes from the life of Aeneas, this privileged environment was designed to welcome and impress even the most distinguished guests of the Pamphilj family. Although the Pamphilj had owned houses on this side of Piazza Navona since the 15th century, it was not until two centuries later that the family had its moment of glory, when Cardinal Giovanni Battista was elected to the pontifical throne as Innocent X in 1644. This taciturn and wary pope was little loved by the public on whom he imposed heavy taxes to satisfy his architectural ambitions. As soon as he became pontiff, he commissioned Girolamo Rainaldi to build this magnificent palace as well as the church of Sant'Agnese in Agone (the family's private chapel), two projects on which Borromini subsequently worked.

The palazzo is also linked to Donna Olimpia Maidalchini, the pope's sister-in-law and one of the most influential women of her time.

An authoritarian and hated figure, all kinds of sordid acts were attributed to her (it was said that she ran Rome's brothels); her ghost is still believed to haunt Piazza Navona. This powerful woman, nicknamed 'Pimpaccia' (a pejorative diminutive of Olimpia) as well as 'she-pope', was probably no worse than her male contemporaries but she was never forgiven for her influence over Innocent X (she was reputed to be his mistress). She was also renowned for her greed – it is said that on the pope's death she stole two chests filled with gold meant for his funeral expenses. In the end, Innocent X was buried without pomp and ceremony in the crypt of Saint Agnes, the place he had built by starving the people.

09.

Palazzo Altemps
Piazza di Sant'Apollinare, 4
Bus 30, 70, 81, 87, 492 – Senato

TOMB OF SAINT ANICETUS

The only pope laid to rest in a private residence

In medieval and Renaissance Rome, being related to a pontiff certainly offered good opportunities for enrichment. Raffaele Sansoni Galeoti Riario was no exception. The nephew of Pope Sixtus IV, he was one of the many fortunate beneficiaries of his eminent uncle, allowing him to build a palace against the walls that ran along Via dei Soldati between the river and what is now Piazza Navona.

Palazzo Riario changed hands several times, with each owner making substantial modifications, before ending up as the property of the German-born Cardinal Mark Sittich von Hohenems, who had Italianised his name to Altemps. The cardinal rebuilt the palace from top to bottom, giving it the form it has today.

A great collector and patron of the arts, he was nevertheless considered an 'upstart' and could not compete with the patrician families whose past was inseparably linked to that of the Eternal City. What then could be better than a saint – if not in the family, at least in your palace – to add a little lustre that might be lacking from your family name?

Pope Clement VIII, who was in Altemps' debt for his unwavering support during his election to the papacy, responded positively to Duke Giovanni Angelo's request to gather the remains of Saint Anicetus, pope and martyr, found in the catacombs of Saint Sebastian in 1602. He had the remains transferred to an antique urn that had, according to tradition, contained the bones of Emperor Severus Alexander. Ever since then, the tomb of Anicetus, the eleventh pope, has lain below the altar in the private chapel of the Altemps family, decorated by Leoni and Pomarancio. This is the only example of a pope laid to rest in a private residence.

WHY IS VIA DEI SOLDATI ('STREET OF THE SOLDIERS') SO NAMED?

Rome was anything but a quiet city. The relentless struggles for influence between the great Roman families quickly degenerated into street brawls and even armed conflict.

They eventually took control over entire neighbourhoods, dividing Rome into many small fiefdoms.

Near the Umberto I bridge over the Tiber was a system of fortifications that separated the Orsinis from the Colonnas. The route patrolled by the militia was thus known as the 'Street of the Soldiers'.

ECCLESIAM ET ALTARE HOC IN HONOREM S. ANICETI P. ET M. SOLEMNITER CONSECRAVIT

10.

Piazza S. Agostino, 8
Bus 30, 70, 81, 87, 492 – Senato

TOUR OF THE ANGELICA LIBRARY

Rome's oldest public library

The Angelica Library (Biblioteca Angelica) is the oldest public library in Rome and one of the first to be founded in Europe. The ensemble has a rare beauty and the enigmatic atmosphere is so hushed that it gives the impression of going back in time.
Book lovers can enjoy these marvellous reading rooms and the precious manuscripts preserved herein during the exhibitions, concerts and guided tours that are regularly organised.
The library is named after an Augustinian bishop, Angelo Rocca, who was in charge of the Vatican printing presses during the pontificate of Sixtus V and left his precious library to the brothers of the convent of Saint Augustine at the end of the 16th century. Rocca wanted anyone to be able to use the library – an outlandish idea at the time.
In 1661, Lukas Holste, then curator of the Vatican library, bequeathed his prodigious collection of printed volumes. In 1762, the acquisition of the books of Cardinal Domenico Passionei doubled this heritage, adding the works that the cardinal had personally acquired during his travels in Protestant countries. This explains why the library contains copies of forbidden texts, the importance of which has been crucial for understanding the Reformation and the Counter-Reformation.
It was around this time that the architect Luigi Vanvitelli was commissioned to restructure the library, particularly its spectacular reading room where scholars still gather today.
Over 200,000 volumes are preserved here, half of which were published between the 15th and the 18th centuries. The most important sections of the library are devoted to the history of the Reformation and the Counter-Reformation and to Augustinian thought, as well as to Dante, Petrarch and Boccaccio, theatre from the 15th to the 18th centuries, Italian and foreign journals of the 17th and 18th centuries, and works on Rome itself. This is also the location of rare books of great artistic value, notably a 9th-century manuscript of the Liber Memorialis from Remiremont Abbey in France, an illuminated codex to Dante's *Divine Comedy* dating from the 14th century, as well as two world maps (maps of the world) from 1603, the only ones in Italy.

Since 1940, the library has also been the headquarters of the Italian literary academy, or Accademia dell'Arcadia.

11.

Piazza Pollarola
Bus 46, 62, 64 – C.So Vittorio Emanuele/S.A. della Valle

THE MARBLE MASK OF PIAZZA POLLAROLA

An old relic of the Theatre of Pompey?

Other than the curvature of via di Grotta Pinta corresponding to the cavea (seating sections) of the theatre, and the straight axis of via dei Chiavari, which marks the place where the stage was, all that remains today of the huge Theatre of Pompey (see opposite) are the vestiges in the basements of the houses built where the theatre once stood. The vaults that supported the seating sections, parts of the walls, and column shafts are visible in several establishments near Campo de' Fiori: the restaurants Da Pancrazio, Le Grotte del Teatro di Pompeo, Largo del Pallaro, and Da Constanza; the Hotel Sole on via del Biscione; the Piazza del Paradiso; and the Teatro di Pompeo hotel.

Both extremities of the complex – the Palazzo Orsini Pio Righetti on Piazza del Biscione, and the Teatro Argentina – were built on top of the ruins of the Temple of Venus Victrix and on those of the curia. A fragment of the curia's foundations was identified in the Area Sacra dell' Argentina. Walled up and declared *locus sceleratus* by Augustus in 32 BCE, the curia was then converted into latrines, probably during Domitian's reign. Many sculptures discovered beneath the courtyard of the Palazzo Righetti – including muses that are said to have decorated the stage wall, satyrs who gave their name to the piazza where they stood, and a gilded bronze statue of Hercules – are kept in the Naples National Archaeological Museum, the Louvre, the Capitoline Museums, and the Pio-Clementino Museum in the Vatican. On a corner wall of Piazza Pollarola, at the second-floor level, hangs a marble mask. It may have been the keystone of one of the building's arches.

THE THEATRE OF POMPEY: THE INFAMOUS PLACE WHERE JULIUS CAESAR WAS MURDERED ?

What is called the Theatre of Pompey is in fact a large architectural complex in the Campus Martius between what is currently Campo de' Fiori and Largo di Torre Argentina. The construction began around 61BCE, ordered by Pompey upon his return from triumphant military campaigns, and was completed in 55 BCE with its inauguration. It was the first permanent theatre built in Rome. Until then, due to fear of political unrest fuelled by popular gatherings, a wooden structure was built every year and dismantled after the games (or ludi). In fact, it has been said that as a ruse, Pompey built the Temple of Venus Victrix above the theatre in order to turn the seating sections of the cavea into the stairs leading to the temple. Standing at 45 metres high, the complex competed with the hills of Rome to the point that it was called an 'architectural hill'. The theatre itself, which could seat 20,000 spectators, only occupied one third of the total area. With their backs to the west, spectators perched up in the seating area – which spanned from the current via del Biscione and via dei Giubbonari for the highest seats to via di Grotta Pinta for the lower seats – looked towards the stage, which would have been where via dei Chiavari is today. To the east, behind the stage wall, a large portico ran all the way to where Largo Torre Argentina currently stands. With its large red granite columns, the portico, which surrounded a garden, was built to protect spectators from adverse weather. It also acted as a museum; adorned with numerous statues, the portico had a rectangular *exedra*, which became the curia, or meeting place, of the Senate. It was in this curia, and not in the curia adjacent to the forum, that Julius Caesar was assassinated on 15 March 44 BCE. Legend has it that he fell at the foot of Pompey's statue. The statue in question (if it is indeed the statue that can be seen today in Palazzo Spada) was found in 1552 in via dei Leutari – in other words, closer to the theatre than to the curia. It is said that the statue could have been standing at the front of the stage, in the same way as Augustus' statue stood above the stage of the Roman Theatre of Orange. Suetonius reported that after Caesar's death, Augustus had the statue moved from the curia – the site of the assassination – to the *regia* (royal door) of the theatre above an arch. Archaeologists now question the authenticity of the statue in Palazzo Spada.

12.

Church of Santa Maria in Monserrato degli Spagnoli
Via di Monserrato, 115
Bus 40, 46, 62, 64 – Chiesa Nuova

THE SAW OF THE CHURCH OF SANTA MARIA IN MONSERRATO DEGLI SPAGNOLI

The shape of the Catalan mountains or a mystical meaning?

Nestled near Piazza Farnese, the entrance portal of the Church of Santa Maria in Monserrato degli Spagnoli – the national church of Spain in Rome – features a striking sculptural group. It depicts the Virgin Mary with the Christ Child cutting into a rock using a saw. This unusual scene explicitly references the renowned Montserrat Sanctuary, a Benedictine monastery in Catalonia. The name *Monserrato* itself means 'serrated mountain', reflecting the dramatic silhouette of jagged rock pinnacles that define this part of the Catalan range.

The act of sawing the rock may also carry a mystical meaning, symbolising the extraordinary power of faith to overcome life's challenges.

Inside the church are significant artefacts linked to Spanish history. The first chapel on the right houses the tombs of two Borgia Popes: Callistus III (1455–1458) and his more famous nephew, Rodrigo, Pope Alexander VI (1492–1503). Nearby, the cenotaph of King Alfonso XIII (1886–1941) commemorates the monarch whose remains were repatriated in 1980 to the Escorial Palace, the grand burial site of Spanish royalty near Madrid.

The church also treasures an early masterpiece by Gian Lorenzo Bernini. In the refectory, a marble portrait of Spanish prelate and jurist Pedro Foix Montoya (1621) showcases the young artist's exceptional talent. At the time of its creation, the portrait gained widespread acclaim, so much so that the commissioner allowed it to remain in Bernini's studio for public admiration. Among its admirers was Maffeo Barberini, later Pope Urban VIII (1623–1644), who would become one of Bernini's most important patrons, propelling him to become a defining figure of the Roman Baroque.

THE FIRST CATHOLIC HOUSE OF WORSHIP IN ROME DESIGNED WITH A SINGLE NAVE

The Church of Santa Maria in Monserrato degli Spagnoli holds the architectural distinction of being the first Catholic church in Rome designed with a single nave. Esteemed architects such as Antonio da Sangallo the Younger and Francesco da Volterra contributed to its construction. It was built on a site previously occupied by hospitals and shelters for pilgrims and the needy, primarily those from the Iberian Peninsula, particularly the Kingdoms of Castile and Aragon.

13.

San Girolamo della Carità,
Via Monserrato, 62 (accès par la piazza S. Caterina della Rota)
Bus 23, 280 – Palazzo Falconieri-Uroboro

CAPPELLA SPADA

Pivoting angel's wings lead to a little-known

Near Piazza Farnese, the church of San Girolamo della Carità is home to an unusual and little-known masterpiece of Baroque art, long attributed to Borromini.
The Spada Chapel is the first on the right on entering the church by the main portal. It was decorated at the request of an influential Oratorian,* Virgilio Spada, who probably commissioned the architect Francesco Righi.
This chapel, whose originality lies in its superb polychrome marble, is separated from the church by a remarkable balustrade designed by Antonio Giorgetti, a pupil of Bernini. It consists of two statues of kneeling angels holding up a great sheet of jasper. Their wings are of wood, and those on the right pivot on hinges to allow access to the chapel. There is not much of note architecturally, but mosaic lovers will be enchanted by the interior. The veined jasper and precious marble suggest damask cloth embroidered with flowers, acanthus leaves, lilies, stars and swords, as if flowing over the floor and the smooth walls of the chapel. The last three of these motifs (lily, star and sword) are the symbols of the Spada family (spada being Italian for sword).
On either side of the altar (a simple block also decorated with mosaics of precious marble) are statues of Bernardino Spada (by Ercole Ferrata) and Giovanni Spada (by Cosimo Fancelli) recumbent on their respective tombs.
Tradition has it that this church was built on the very spot where the house of the widow Paula (who, in the 4th century CE, gave shelter to Saint Jerome) once stood. This was the house that Domenico Castelli rebuilt around the mid-17th century.
Before leaving the church, do not overlook the small and beautiful Antamoro chapel to the left of the high altar, the only work in Rome by Filippo Juvarra, and the statue of Saint Philip Néri by Pierre Legros.

** Member of the Congregation of Saint Philip Néri.*

SAINT PHILIP NÉRI'S CELL AT SAN GIROLAMO DELLA CARITÀ

Saint Philip lived for some 30 years in the convent of San Girolamo della Carità (an annex of the church). His cell, which has been turned into a chapel, can still be seen.

14.

Via Giulia, 262, at via dei Farnesi
Bus 23, 280 – Palazzo Falconieri-Uroboro

HYPOGEUM CEMETERY OF SANTA MARIA DELL'ORAZIONE E MORTE CHURCH

'My turn today, yours tomorrow'

The church of Santa Maria dell'Orazione e Morte, seat of the arch brotherhood of the same name, overlooks Via Giulia opposite the Farnese arch. The façade bears a plaque featuring a skeleton who warns passers-by: *Hodie mihi, cras tibi* (literally, 'Today for me, tomorrow for you').

Inside, having noted the decorations rich in necrological symbols, you enter the crypt via the sacristy, to the left of the high altar. You can also visit the remains of the ancient cemetery, the greater part of which was destroyed around 1870 during the construction of the barrier walls along the Tiber, the river waters having flooded the cells on more than one occasion. Two plaques still indicate the different levels that the water had reached inside the cemetery.

From 1552 to 1896, the brotherhood gathered over 8,000 bodies, a fair number of which were buried in this crypt. Wherever a body was found without a grave, in the depths of a bog, thrown up by the Tiber or the sea, or lying in the brush, the members of the brotherhood would recover it for holy burial.

Today, these galleries are like a boneyard in which the decorative artwork, crosses, sculptures and lamps have been made from bones and skeletons. In addition, the name of the deceased has been engraved on certain exposed skulls, with the date and sometimes the cause of death together with the place where the body was found.

15.

Accademia d'Ungheria (Hungarian Academy)
Via Giulia, 1
Bus 62 – C.So Vittorio Emanuele/Navona

ESOTERIC SYMBOLS AT PALAZZO FALCONIERI

Alchemy among the Falconieri

Along the quiet Via Giulia, next to the church of Santa Maria dell'Orazione e Morte (Saint Mary of Prayer and Death), curious figures with a falcon's head and woman's breasts stand guard over Palazzo Falconieri. They are probably by Francesco Borromini, who in 1646 designed the beautiful three-arched loggia facing the Tiber.

The falcon's head is a dual allusion to the name Orazio Falconieri, who rebuilt the palace in the 17th century: the falcon was the symbol of the Falconieri (Italian for 'falconers') family of Florentine origin; and the Egyptian god Horus (falcon-headed) recalled the name Orazio.

The figure of the falcon with its apparently female breasts is also an alchemical symbol of the 'mercurial water' used in philosophical distillation in which the metal is washed to purify it (phase of alchemical sublimation).

Borromini also left his mark on the ceilings of the four salons on the first floor, decorated in stuccowork with symbolic elements of great complexity that fit into the alchemical tradition. The stuccos, which were originally in monochrome, were coloured in 1781 on the occasion of the marriage of Costanza Falconieri.

In the red salon, three intersecting laurel wreaths at the centre, traversed by sunbeams, symbolise the Trinity.

In the blue salon, the central oval shows a globe set upon the Earth with a sceptre arising from it (the axis of the world) and surmounted by an all-seeing eye (God). Behind the globe is the Ouroboros (tail-devouring snake), symbol of the eternal cycle of nature and the universal manifestation of God, and a laurel wreath signifying the union of heaven (God) and Earth (man).

The last two salons, which are both green, have elegant decorations inspired by plant life.

Visitors should definitely go out onto the terrace for a magnificent view over the city, including the nearby gardens of Palazzo Farnese.

Palazzo Falconieri, which was the residence of Cardinal Fesch in the early 19th century, has been the seat of the Hungarian Academy since 1927.

For more information about the ouroboros, see the following double page.

THE OUROBOROS: A SYMBOL OF DIVINE ILLUMINATION

The figure of a coiled serpent biting its own tail is sometimes found in iconography and literature. This symbol is traditionally known as the Ouroboros, a Greek word derived from the Coptic and Hebrew languages – *ouro* is Coptic for 'king' and *ob* is Hebrew for 'serpent' – meaning 'royal serpent'. Thus the reptile raising its head above its body is used as a symbol of mystical illumination: for Eastern peoples, it represents the divine fire they call Kundalini. Kundalini is the origin of the association that Western medicine of the Middle Ages and Renaissance made between, on the one hand, the body heat that rises from the base of the spine to the top of the head and, on the other, the *venena bibas* ('ingested venom' mentioned by Saint Benedict of Nursia) of the snake whose bite can only be treated by an equally potent poison. Just as the Eastern techniques of spiritual awakening, Dzogchen and Mahamudra, show how a meditating person must learn to 'bite his tail like the serpent', the theme of the Ouroboros and ingested venom is a reminder that spiritual awareness can only result from a devout life: by elevating your consciousness onto a mental plane surpassing the ordinary, you search within to truly find yourself as an eternal being. The Greeks popularised the word *ouroboros* in its literal sense of 'serpent biting its tail'. They acquired this image from the Phoenicians through contact with the Hebrews, who had themselves adopted it from Egypt where the Ouroboros featured on a stele dated as early as 1600 BCE. There it represented the sun god Ra (Light), who resurrects life from the darkness of the night (synonymous with death), going back to the theme of eternal return, life, death, and the renewal of existence, as well as the reincarnation of souls in successive human bodies until they have reached their evolutionary peak, which will leave them perfect, both physically and spiritually – a theme dear to Eastern peoples. In this sense, the serpent swallowing itself can also be interpreted as an interruption of the cycle of human development (represented by the serpent) in order to enter the cycle of spiritual evolution (represented by the circle). Pythagoras associated the serpent with the mathematical concept of infinity, coiled up as zero – the abstract number used to denote eternity, which becomes reality when the Ouroboros is depicted turning around on itself. Gnostic Christians identified it with the Holy Spirit revealed through wisdom to be the Creator of all things visible and invisible, and whose ultimate expression on Earth is Christ. For this reason, the symbol is associated in Greek Gnostic literature with the phrase *hen to pan* ('The All is One'); it was commonly adopted in the 4th and 5th centuries as a protective amulet against evil spirits and venomous snakebites. This amulet was known as Abraxas, the name of a god in the original Gnostic pantheon that the Egyptians recognised as Serapis. It became one of the most famous magical talismans of the Middle Ages. Greek alchemists very quickly espoused the figure of the Ouroboros (or Uroboros) and so it reached the Hermetic philosophers of Alexandria – among them, Arab thinkers who studied and disseminated this image in their schools of Hermeticism and alchemy. These schools were known and sought out by medieval Christians. There is even historical evidence that members of the Order of the Knights Templar, as well as other Christian mystics, travelled to Cairo, Syria and even Jerusalem to be initiated into the Hermetic sciences.

Mausoleo di Augusto
Piazza di Spagna
Trinità dei Monti
PIAZZA AUGUSTO IMPERATORE
PIAZZA DI SPAGNA
PIAZZA DELLA TRINITÀ DEI MONTI
Palazzo Borghese
LARGO FONTANELLA BORGHESE
PIAZZA SAN LORENZO IN LUCIA
PIAZZA MIGNANELLI
COLONNA
PIAZZA DEL PARLAMENO
PIAZZA SAN SILVESTRO
PIAZZA DI FIRENZE
PIAZZA DI CAMPO MARZIO
TREVI
Fontana di Trevi
PIAZZA DI MONTECITORIO
PIAZZA COLONNA
PIAZZA DELLA MADDALENA
PIAZZA CAPRANICA
PIAZZA DI PIETRA
PIAZZA DI TREVI
PIAZZA DELLA ROTONDA
PIAZZA SANT'IGNAZIO
Palazzo del Quirinale
PIAZZA DEL QUIRINALE
Pantheon
PIAZZA DELLA PILOTTA
PIAZZA DELLA MINERVA
Santa Maria Sopra Minerva
PIAZZA COLLEGIO ROMANO
PIAZZA SANTISSIMI APOSTOLI
Galleria Colonna
PIAZZA DELLA PIGNA
PIAZZA GRAZIOLI
Palazzo Doria Pamphilj
LARGO DI TORRE ARGENTINA
PIAZZA VENEZIA
LARGO MAGNANAPOLI
PIAZZA DEL GESÙ
Gesù
CAPITOL
AREA SACRA DI LARGO ARGENTINA
PIAZZA SAN MARCO
Colonna Traiana
LARGO ARENULA
Altare della Patria
Palazzo Mattei
PIAZZA MARGANA
PIAZZA MATTEI
PIAZZA D'ARACŒLI
Santa Maria in Aracœli
PIAZZA COSTAGUTI
ANGELO
PIAZZA CAPIZUCCHI
PIAZZA DI CAMPITELLI
PIAZZA DEL CAMPIDOGLIO
Curia
FORO ROMANO
Teatro di Marcello
Tevere
PONTE FABRICIO
PIAZZA MONTE SAVELLO
PIAZZA DELLA CONSOLAZIONE
ISOLA TIBERINA
PONTE CESTIO
0 100 200 m
N

CENTRE SOUTH

01.

Colonna Gallery
Piazza dei Santi Apostoli, 66
Metro A – Spagna or B – Colosseo

PRINCESS ISABELLE'S APARTMENT

A fantastic private visit

The gallery of Palazzo Colonna is certainly one of the most precious of Italy's artistic treasures and only insiders know that since 1946 it has been open to visitors once a week. Its extraordinary beauty can be enjoyed on Saturday mornings, by going through a small entrance hidden in the beautiful Via della Pilotta. Nor do many people know that while on private visits to the gallery, you can gain access to the rest of the palace.

By contacting the palace administration and booking a private visit, it is possible to admire, alone and undisturbed, parts of the palace that are closed to the public: the gallery, a series of adjacent rooms and the apartment of Princess Isabelle Sursock Colonna, who lived here until the end of the 1980s. This last visit is a unique experience: in the rooms of the apartment facing the interior garden some extraordinary art is to be found, such as the frescoes by the renowned painter Bernardino di Betto, known as Pinturicchio, refined works of Flemish masters, including engravings by Jan Bruegel the Elder, the rich collection of views by Gaspard Van Wittel, known in Italy as di Vanvitelli, and the decorations of Gaspard Dughet, Crescenzio Onofri, Cavalier Tempesta, Giacinto Gimignani and Carlo Cesi.

THE PALAZZO COLONNA CANNON BALL

Fired from the Janiculum Hill during a confrontation between French troops and Garibaldi's soldiers defending the Roman Republic in 1849, a cannon ball can amazingly still be seen on the grand staircase linking the two levels of the Palazzo Colonna gallery.

The projectile shattered one of the great windows and flew across the gallery before wedging itself in the steps, where the palace owners have left it as a reminder of the incident.

02.

Church of the Twelve Holy Apostles
Piazza dei Santi Apostoli, 51
Metro A – Spagna or B – Colosseo

CARDINAL BESSARION'S CHAPEL

The most important set of paintings of the Roman Quattrocento

Located at the heart of the Church of the Twelve Holy Apostles, the funerary chapel of Cardinal Bessarion – open to the public since 2008 after a long period of restoration – was not found by accident alone. During restoration works in 1959 in the adjacent Palazzo Colonna, a wall was breached, revealing a fantastic set of frescoes painted by Antoniazzo Romano and Melozzo da Forlì. These frescoes are considered the most important set of paintings of the Roman Quattrocento.

The works are closely linked to the history of Christianity. Indeed, at the time of his instigation, Cardinal Bessarion (originally from Trebizond on the Black Sea), in agreement with the Byzantine Emperor John VIII Palaiologos, and under the auspices of Pope Eugene IV, made great efforts to reunite the Orthodox and Catholic churches in order to repel the threat of a Turkish invasion. It was with this aim in mind that the Council of Ferrara was held in 1438. The following year, the council was moved to Florence to avoid the plague in Ferrara. However, after failing to reach an agreement, the unification of the Greek and Latin churches never materialised and Constantinople fell in 1453.

Cardinal Bessarion worked tirelessly to protect Greek artists and thinkers exiled in Constantinople. He contributed to salvaging a great number of ancient Greek manuscripts (all of which were given to Venice and form the nucleus of the Marciana library) and never stopped dreaming of taking back Constantinople. This was the wish he wanted to express in his funerary chapel.

In 1465 Cardinal Bessarion entrusted the responsibility of this project to painter Antoniazzo Romano, a specialist in the reproduction of Eastern Christian icons, which were particularly fashionable at the time due to the influence of the many Byzantine artists who took refuge in Rome. Antoniazzo completed the 'Madonna with Child' – now displayed on the chapel's lower level (accessible by a metal staircase) – and had his assistants help him create the frescoes depicting the allegory of Saint Michael's battle against evil, in all their fresh and splendid colours.

The right side shows the apparition of Saint Michael in France, while the left side represents his apparition in Italy (Mount Gargano). In the background, as a clear symbol of *rapprochement* between the Orthodox and Catholic churches, Franciscan monks wearing garments made of frieze stand beside Basilian monks (Eastern church) in black robes. But the most interesting element is the reference to France, which, at the time, was the country most capable of leading this ultimate crusade. The painter thus gave Saint Aubert, the bishop of Avranches and founder of the Mont-Saint-Michel Abbey, who is seen wearing his mitre and ceremonial robes, the traits of Louis XI. The characters standing behind the bishop were given the traits of Francesco della Rovere, the future Pope Sixtus IV (wearing red cardinal's robes), and Giuliano della Rovere, the future Pope Julius II (in a purple robe). Through Antoniazzo, Bessarion urged the entire Christian world to the Crusade.

On the scene to the right, the Mont-Saint-Michel Abbey is visible in the background; the shells depicted by the painter on the seafront are there to signal the low tide granting access to the abbey.

Cardinal Bessarion lived in the palazzo adjacent to the Church of the Twelve Holy Apostles. On the palazzo's façade, near the left angle, under the cornice of the first floor, is a bas-relief of ribbons, which would appear to refer to a cardinal's hat. In all probability they refer not to Bessarion but to the Colonna family, who provided the church with a plethora of cardinals (including one who became pope under the name Martin V) for who this palazzo was reserved. It temporarily became the property of Cardinal Bessarion before returning to the Colonna family. Today it houses the Order of Friars Minor Conventual, and despite its two magnificent cloister/courtyards, it cannot be visited.

The cardinal owned a suburban villa – one of the first in the Renaissance – located at number 8 via di Porta San Sebastiano, at the beginning of the via Appia. There, he welcomed all the intellectuals of his time, especially Greek scholars and artists who had fled Constantinople. The modest and charming villa is decorated with frescoes and surrounded by a garden. Make an appointment to visit the villa by contacting the association Genti e Paesi (06 85 30 17 58).

03.

Church of the Twelve Holy Apostles
Piazza dei Santi Apostoli, 51
Metro A – Spagna or B – Colosseo

HIDDEN MESSAGE OF THE HOLY APOSTLES

A discreet tribute to spare the pope's susceptibilities

The ancient basilica of the Holy Apostles has been altered several times, even rebuilt, and Pope Sixtus IV added the imposing portico that opens onto the square. It is now crowned with 13 statues of Jesus and the Apostles.
A letter is engraved on the pedestal of each statue, forming a strange series as these letters do not use the traditional abbreviations found on ancient monuments and, *a priori*, have no connection with the figures of the saints above.

The series of letters (F L D L C S O T C E C V B) is actually a 'tribute' to Cardinal Lorenzo Brancati di Lauria, tutor at the monastery of Santi Apostoli, who donated the sculptures.
This theologian, who was close to Pope Alexander VII and adviser to the 'Congregation of the Apostolic Visitation', was librarian at the Vatican and he commissioned and paid for the statues.
Although his gift was probably disinterested, as the donor he still wished to go down in posterity, so rather than having an inscription that was too ostentatious or self-serving and might have hurt the pontifical feelings, he devised this little puzzle:
Frater Laurentius De Laureolo Consultor Sancti Officii Theologus Cardinalis Episcopus Custos Vaticanae Bibliothecae (Brother Lorenzo de Laureolo, adviser and theologian of the Holy Office, cardinal, bishop, librarian of the Vatican library).

Michelangelo was laid to rest for a time at Santi Apostoli before his tomb was moved to the basilica of Santa Croce in Florence, which is a sort of pantheon to 'illustrious Italians'.

E

04.

Via di San Marcello
Metro A – Spagna or B – Colosseo

SANCTUARY OF OUR LADY OF THE SMALL ARCH

Virgin's eyes

A short distance from the Trevi Fountain, hidden from the casual glance, the unusual chapel dedicated to *Madonna dell'Archetto* (Our Lady of the Small Arch) is the smallest Marian sanctuary in the city.
The narrow street that joined Via di San Marcello to Via dell'Archetto had a picture of the Virgin Mary painted on its wall. Domenico Muratori, a painter from Bologna and a student of Carracci, painted this picture for the marchioness Savorelli Papazzurri in 1690.
In 1696, the Virgin miraculously moved her eyes and the owner decided to display her within the street's arch for public veneration. In 1751, it was decided to close the entrances to the street with two gates, in order to protect the precious offerings that had accumulated. In 1796, the miracle, which was witnessed by several people, took place again and was recognised by the Church. In the middle of the 19th century, the street was finally closed off completely and made into a chapel. The Savorelli Papazzurri family commissioned the architect Virginio Vespignani to build a small sanctuary, a jewel of neo-Renaissance art. It was solemnly inaugurated on 31 May 1851. The small temple, declared a national art monument and yet relatively unknown, contains sculptures by Luigi Simonetti and encaustic paintings by Costantino Brumidi, who, using the same technique, also painted the *Apotheosis of George Washington* fresco and became known as the 'Michelangelo of the United States Capitol'.

05.

Palazzo di Montecitorio
Piazza di Montecitorio
Metro A – Barberini

THE WINDOW SILLS OF THE PALAZZO DI MONTECITORIO

The importance of rough stone in Bernini's art

Though they protrude ever so slightly from their original gangue on the south-east and south-west angles of the Palazzo di Montecitorio, the strange window sills that seem to have been carved directly from the rock are rarely noticed by visitors. Fragments of leaves and twigs also appear in the carving, as though the stone was alive. Far from being a mistake or an unfinished element, these sills were an intentional choice on Bernini's part, even though they were created by Carlo Fontana. The construction of the palace was commissioned from Bernini by Pope Innocent X in 1653 for one of his nephews, Niccolò Ludovisi. However, work was put on hold for nearly 50 years until Pope Innocent XII entrusted the completion of the building to Carlo Fontana, one of Bernini's students.

Fontana kept the Baroque style of the huge convex façade and the angular windows, where the unexpected and artificial vie for attention. Also carved so as to appear rough and unfinished, the building's angles allude to nature's untamed energy bursting out from architectural order. Alternatively, as more politically inclined minds would have it, the technique represents nature's submission to papal order.

The use of rough stone is a recurring element in Bernini's art; he used it profusely in the Piazza Navona, where the obelisk bearing the papal coat of arms already towered above an artificial rock base. Pope Innocent X – with whom Bernini had fallen out of favour for having been the official architect and sculptor of Pope Urban VIII, his predecessor – found the fountain particularly charming and commissioned Bernini to design Palazzo di Montecitorio, which was then called Ludovisi.

Ten years later, Bernini drew on this theme again in his project for the Louvre; his plan was to elevate the building above a rocky foundation as he had done for the obelisk of his 'Fountain of the Four Rivers'. However, Louis XIV had other plans.

HOSPITII APOSTOLICI
INVALIDORVM

06.

Piazza Sant'Eustachio,
Bus 30, 70, 81, 87 – Rinascimento

THE STAG OF SANT'EUSTACHIO CHURCH

A stag's head in place of Christ's cross

A vigilant pedestrian looking upwards in Piazza Sant'Eustachio might notice a curious detail: instead of the traditional Christian cross that surmounts churches, the world over, the church of Sant'Eustachio is crowned with a stag's head, with a cross on top of it. This curiosity owes its existence to the life of St Eustace, who converted to Christianity when he encountered a stag with a crucifix between its antlers.

ST EUSTACE

Martyred in Rome around 130 CE, St Eustace was originally named Placidus. After his conversion he took the name Eustace (Latin Eustachius), which signifies 'constancy'. His feast day is 20 September, believed to be the day of his death.

On his way to hunt in the forest one day, Placidus, a well-respected Roman soldier, came across a herd of deer, one of which seemed larger and more splendid than the others. He approached the herd to kill the stag and noticed that he bore a crucifix in his antlers. A divine voice spoke to the soldier, saying that it had come to save him. In the face of this miracle, and because his wife had had a similar dream the night before, the whole family was baptized.

Returning the next morning to the scene of the miracle, Eustace once again had a vision of Christ, who informed the saint that he was going to be put to the test but that Christ would never forsake him. A few days later, plague overwhelmed the region. St Eustace lost his troops and his home was raided. He and his family fled to Egypt. His wife was held for ransom by the owner of the boat making the crossing, but Eustace journeyed on with his two children who were soon taken by wild animals, one by a lion and the other by a wolf. After some years, the family was finally reunited. His wife had not after all been defiled by the boat's captain, and the children had been saved by villagers. After refusing to sacrifice to pagan gods, however, the family was put to death by the Emperor Hadrian.

07.

Via della Spada di Orlando
Bus 51, 62, 63, 83, 85, 119, 160 – Corso/Minghetti

SCAR ON A MARBLE COLUMN

Mark left by Roland of Roncesvalles' sword

A small street leading into Piazza Capranica, near the Pantheon, bears traces of the knight Roland (Orlando in Italian) when he passed through Rome.
Actually, it's more than just a trace: it's a 'scar' left by his legendary sword Durandal on a marble column.

Charlemagne's paladin, who was visiting the city, was engaged in a brawl with some Roman knights. Given their number, Roland was forced to draw his sword – his attackers soon fled.
During the fight, one of his blows struck a block of marble and split it in two.
Today it is still easy to imagine Durandal's magical powers – or Roland's strength – in this little street that was subsequently named 'Street of the Sword of Roland'.

This marble column belongs to a larger group which includes the remains of a nearby ancient wall, clearly visible where it slightly encroaches on the street from the overhanging medieval building. These are the ruins of the Temple of Matidia, built by Emperor Hadrian in 119 CE in honour of his mother-in-law. Two other columns, an impressive 1.7 metres in diameter and 17 metres high, are incorporated in the façade of the house at No. 17 Piazza Capranica.

08.

Sacristy of the Church of St. Ignatius of Loyola
Piazza Sant'Ignazio
Bus 51, 62, 63, 83, 85, 119, 160 – Corso/Minghetti

THE ROOMS OF SAINT ALOYSIUS DE GONZAGA

A true Jesuit secret

Given that the rooms, or cappelletti, of Saint Aloysius de Gonzaga – located in the sacristy of the Church of St Ignatius – are accessible by appointment only, they are relatively unknown even to Romans. And yet, on the last floor of the Collegio Romano, adjacent to the church, is a room called the *Ritiramento*. Here, for nearly two centuries, Jesuit students, including the young Aloysius de Gonzaga, used to live. These rooms were originally very simple, but over time, as the rite of beatification (and Aloysius de Gonzaga's popularity) grew, the rooms were embellished. They were restored several times during the 18th century, and again very recently. Aloysius was born in 1568. As the eldest son of Ferrante de Gonzaga, Marquis of Castiglione delle Stiviere, he was destined for a career in the military. At the age of nine he took a vow of chastity in the Basilica della Santissima Annunziata in Florence. During his time as a page boy at the court of Philip II, young Gonzaga developed a strong aversion to life at court. At 17 he entered the Society of Jesus against his father's will. He left for Rome and began his university studies at the Roman College. It was during his studies that he occupied the room that has since been restored and embellished, and in which a statue can be found representing him trampling an upturned crown as he contemplates the crucifix. The trampled crown symbolises his renunciation of his rights of inheritance to the Duchy of Mantua in favour of his younger brother Rodolfo. The crucifix, a central element in Jesuit spirituality, is still found in the saint's iconography today. In 1591 Rome suffered an epidemic of plague. Jesuits dedicated their time to helping the sick, and Aloysius was seen carrying a plague victim on his back. A few days later, on 21 June 1591, Aloysius himself died of the plague at just 23 years old. His body was buried in the chapel of the right transept of the church of Saint Ignatius of Loyola. Blessed in 1604 by Pope Clement VIII, he was then canonised in 1726 by Pope Benedict XIII, who declared him the patron saint of young students. In 1926 Pope Pius XI declared Aloysius de Gonzaga to be the patron of all Christian youth.

THE CHURCH OF SANT'IGNAZIO

Founded by Cardinal Ludovisi in 1626 and built in phases until 1662, the Church of Sant'Ignazio has a peculiar aspect that goes unnoticed by most visitors: the cupola, whose decoration and dimensions appear to be unexceptional at first glance, was never actually built due to technical problems. The dome, which is flat, was painted in trompe-l'œil fashion by Father Andrea Pozzo. His Glory of Saint Ignatius was painted in the nave's vault with impressive perspective. The effect is strange as you walk from the centre of the nave to the altar while admiring the cupola's skylight: the initial perspective wanes and you realise there is, in fact, no cupola.

09.

Via del Collegio Romano, 27
Bus 51, 62, 63, 83, 85, 119, 160 – Corso/Minghetti

THE MONUMENTAL HALL OF COLLEGIO ROMANO

An exceptional, little-known library

Lovers of art or archaeology, ancient books and great Baroque library enthusiasts will take great pleasure in exploring the spectacular Sala Crociera (cruciform hall) of Collegio Romano, or even studying in the sumptuous reading room attached to it.

The immense hall in the form of a cross, as its name indicates, is disconcertingly beautiful. The walls that form the arms of the cross are entirely covered in books, most of them ancient and rare. The superb shelving where they are stacked was built especially for the library in the 17th century, at the time when the hall was the main library of the college founded by Saint Ignatius of Loyola and modelled on the University of Paris.

More recently, this hall and the adjoining reading room were part of the National Library of Rome, until the latter moved into its present site at Castro Pretorio.

Since 1989, these halls have been occupied by the Library of Archaeology and History of Art, and the collection includes a vast number of volumes donated by archaeologists, art and architecture historians, as well as a collection of art gallery catalogues, with sections devoted to theatre, music, heraldry and Oriental art, besides an exceptional collection of catalogues from the principal salerooms dating from the 19th century onwards.

10.

Collegio Romano
Piazza del Collegio romano, 4
Bus 51, 62, 63, 83, 85, 119, 160 – Corso/Minghetti

MUSEO ATHANASIUS KIRCHER

Remains of a fantastic cabinet of curiosities

The Roman College was built between 1582 and 1584 by the architect Bartolomeo Ammannati (although some attribute it to the Jesuit Giuseppe Valeriani), thanks to Pope Gregory XIII, the 'founding father and protector' of the institution. It was the seat of one of the largest universities of Baroque Rome, inspired by the free school of grammar and Christian doctrine conceived in 1551 by Ignatius of Loyola, founder of the Jesuits. Today the buildings are shared by the Visconti high school, the Ministry of Culture and the research unit for climatology and meteorology.

Among its teachers, the college – which was witness to the learned debates between Galileo and Segneri – counted scientists such as Clavius, who helped draw up the Gregorian calendar, and Athanasius Kircher, polymath and creator in 1651 of a Wunderkammer, a cabinet of curiosities that was famous throughout Europe. In the Athanasius Kircher Museum works of art rubbed shoulders with scientific instruments, specimens from the natural world and all kinds of rare and curious objects, such as a stone from the tower of Babel, obviously of rather dubious authenticity.

The collections were dispersed for the first time during the suppression of the Jesuits (1773) and were then scattered throughout various Roman museums during the fascist era. Today only a fraction of them can be seen in the small high-school museum that was opened in 1870 and enriched by acquisitions of the 18th and 19th centuries. The great hall houses mineralogical and natural specimens (such as the skeleton of a newborn child), most of which came from the Antonio Neviani's collection.

A room on the top floor has an interesting collection of scientific instruments, an 18th-century sperm pouch (!) and most notably the six wooden obelisks used by Kircher to illustrate his Egyptology lessons. Three of these are faithful scale models of the obelisks at the Lateran, Flaminio and Villa Medici. The fourth is an invention of Kircher's and bears a dedication to Pope Clement IX, beneath which an earlier dedication to Queen Christina of Sweden has been found. The other two obelisks have no inscriptions. As a known expert on the subject, Kircher collaborated with Bernini on the Fontana dei Quattro Fiumi (Fountain of the Four Rivers) in Piazza Navona and was convinced he had found the secret of interpreting hieroglyphs.

11.

Via Sant'Ignazio, 52
Bus 51, 62, 63, 83, 85, 119, 160 – Corso/Minghetti

CASANATENSE LIBRARY

A sumptuous monumental hall

With the exception of employees and a few researchers, hardly anyone knows that the sumptuous Casanatense Library is open regularly to the public for exhibitions, conferences, performances and concerts, and can even be visited free of charge upon request.

This library was founded by the Dominican friars of the Monastery of Santa Maria sopra Minerva in Rome at the request of Cardinal Girolamo Casanate, and inaugurated in 1701 in a structure within the Minerva cloister specially designed by the architect A. M. Borioni.

To the 25,000 original volumes that the cardinal bequeathed to the library were added many others acquired by the Dominicans over the years. Through their contacts with the main European booksellers, they sought out both antique and modern volumes to build up a 'universal library' of texts on theology, economics and Roman law, as well as other scientific and artistic works.

In 1884, the Dominican librarians were finally replaced by civil servants when the library was forfeited to the Italian state. Since then it has formed part of the Ministry of Culture with a collection of over 350,000 works.

The splendid *salone* (hall), measuring 60.15 by 15.30 metres, is home to some 55,000 illustrated works dating from the 16th to the 18th centuries, displayed on magnificent wooden shelves built by the sculptor Marchesi and the gilder Cantoni to a design by Borioni.

The shelving, divided by a single gallery halfway up, covers the walls from floor to ceiling, bathed in a perfectly uniform flood of light from the windows pierced in the vaulting above. The coat of arms of the Casanate family can be seen (a tower surmounted by an eight-pointed star), the same symbol found on the library decorations and stamped on each object in the collection. This includes two magnificent 18th-century globes (the Earth and the Heavens), drawn in pen and wash by Abbot Moroncelli, a celebrated cosmographer, geographer and topographer, as well as an ancient copper armillary sphere surmounting the statue of Cardinal Casanate, created in 1708 by the French sculptor Pierre Le Gros.

12.

Piazza della Minerva
Bus 30, 40, 62, 64, 81, 87, 492 – Largo di Torre Argentina

THE HIDDEN SYMBOLISM OF BERNINI'S ELEPHANT-OBELISK

A symbol of the resurrection of the body

Although Bernini's curious elephant-obelisk is of course famous in Rome, its symbolism is much less well-known. Why did Bernini design such an unusual sculpture? What does it signify? Bernini's design for the base of the obelisk, a stone elephant, is very similar to an engraving that appeared in Hypnerotomachia Poliphili [Poliphilo's Dream of the Strife of Love], the extraordinary Renaissance roman à clef published in Venice in 1499 (portraying well-known real people disguised as fictional characters – see the following double-page spread). While for the Egyptians, the obelisk symbolised the 'divine rays of the Sun', the great mass of the elephant symbolised the Earth. With its trunk, it draws up water (the rain) which flows through the interior; the Earth is nourished, and with the help of the Sun (the obelisk) which traverses the Earth (the elephant), the grain is fertilised, so that it can be reborn and flourish. In the text that inspired Bernini, the reader enters the elephant, inside of which a man and a woman are represented. The full force of the symbol is thus revealed: besides the grain which is reborn and fertilised, the elephant-obelisk symbolises the resurrection of the body, a belief transmitted by the Egyptians (notably in the Book of the Dead) to the Hebrews and Christians to become a central element of Christianity. At the Last Judgment (like the biblical Jonah who emerges from the belly of the whale), man will leave the Earth to rise again from the dead. Pope Alexander VII, who commissioned the monument from Bernini in 1667 to be erected on the site of a former Temple of Isis, possessed a copy (annotated in his own hand) of Hypnerotomachia Poliphili and it was he who had the Latin phrase inscribed on the base recalling the immense wisdom passed down from ancient Egypt.* Remember that in Christian doctrine, the resurrection of Christ foreshadows that of all men and women at the Last Judgment. Finally, the Bernini sculpture also bears an eight-pointed star. The figure 8, for Christians, is the symbol of resurrection.

* *Sapientis Ægypti / insculptas obelisco figuras / ab elephanto / belluarum fortissima / gestari quisquis hic vides / documentum intellige / robustae mentis esse / solidam sapientiam sustinere* [These symbols of the science of Egypt, which you see engraved on the obelisk borne by the elephant, the most powerful of all animals, take them as the precept that a strong mind is needed to support a solid knowledge]

There is another elephant bearing an Egyptian obelisk at Catania in Sicily.

POLIPHILO'S DREAM OF THE STRIFE OF LOVE, AN EXTRAORDINARY HUMANIST ROMANCE THAT DIRECTLY INSPIRED THE GARDENS OF VERSAILLES, BOBOLI (FLORENCE) AND BERNINI'S CELEBRATED ELEPHANT-OBELISK

Printed by Aldus Manutius in Venice in 1499, *Hypnerotomachia Poliphili* [*Poliphilo's Dream of the Strife of Love*] is perhaps the most complex *roman-à-clef* ever published.

Illustrated with around 170 exquisite woodcuts, it is also considered one of the finest examples of early printing.

The book, written in a mixture of Italian, Latin, Greek, Hebrew, Arabic, Spanish, Venetian and a few other dialects, was long considered anonymous. Recent research, however, chiefly led by Emanuela Kretzulesco, has pointed to Francesco Colonna, as the decorative first letters of each of the 38 chapters spell out the following phrase: *Poliam Frater Franciscus Columna peramavit* ('Brother Francesco Colonna dearly loved Polia').

A nephew of Cardinal Prospero Colonna, Francesco Colonna was part of the circle of Enlightenment figures that included Cardinal Bessarion, the future Pope Pius II and Nicholas V, known as the Renaissance Pope, opposed to the succeeding popes and in particular to Alexander VI Borgia.

At a time when the Borgias, against the advice of Pius II and Nicholas V, were seeking to grant the pontiff temporal as well as spiritual power, and the papacy was embarking on a dark period of its history, *Poliphilo's Dream* was consequently rendered deliberately obscure in order to escape papal censure.

More than a story of Poliphilo's love for Lucrezia, the book is a spiritual quest of a philosopher passionately devoted to divine wisdom (Athena Polias). Developing humanist themes, he transmitted in a cryptic way the spiritual testament of a circle of theologians united around Nicholas V, who had undertaken comparative studies of religious traditions going back to ancient Greece and Egypt with great openness of mind, thus reviving the heritage of Pope Sylvester II (Gerbert of Aurillac).

In concurrence with the Florentine Platonic Academy of the Medici and Marsilio Ficino, this group notably included the architect Leon Battista Alberti and Prospero Colonna, as well as being a great inspiration to Pico della Mirandola, Leonardo da Vinci, Nicolaus Copernicus, Giordano Bruno and Galileo. *Poliphilo's Dream* reveals that the best way to know God is through Nature, divine creation. With the help of the codes held in the *Hieroglyphica* of Horus Apollo (Horapollo), it also illuminates the spiritual road that leads there.

In an absolutely extraordinary fashion for anyone interested in understanding the background against which *Poliphilo's Dream* evolved, it is clear that it also closely inspired the gardens of Versailles or Boboli in Florence, as well as Bernini's celebrated elephant-obelisk in Rome through the numerous symbols scattered along *Poliphilo*'s route.

WHAT DOES *HYPNEROTOMACHIA* MEAN?

The etymology of the term Hypnerotomachia is based on the following Greek words: *hypnos* (sleep), *eros* (love), and *mache* (fight).

THE UNREQUITED LOVE OF LORENZO DE' MEDICI: AN INSPIRATION FOR POLIPHILO AND SHAKESPEARE?

The doomed love affair of Lorenzo de' Medici and Lucrezia Donati (who was married to Niccolò Ardinghelli against her will) seems to have directly inspired Poliphilo's quest: same name, same events, same timescale (1462–1464)... The love life of Lorenzo the Magnificent is also thought to have provided the material for Francesco Cei, a poet close to Lorenzo, in his poem *Giulia e Romeo*, which directly inspired Shakespeare to write the famous *Romeo and Juliet*.

13.

Palazzo Berardi
Via del Gesù, 62
Bus 30, 40, 62, 64, 81, 87, 492 – Largo di Torre Argentina

BERARDI'S WATER CLOCK

A rare and curious mechanism

Stop in front of the open gate of Palazzo Berardi, in the La Pigna district, to see a superb and theatrical water clock (hydrochronometer) in the courtyard.
It was installed in 1870 by the Dominican scholar Giovan Battista Embriaco, head of the nearby Minerva convent. The clock was not his first attempt, as he had already successfully presented two prototypes at the Paris Universal Exposition of 1867.
This curious mechanism, which is still in working order, sits at the centre of a shell surrounded by four caryatids supporting two marble busts. The whole structure acts as a fountain and water feature.

14.

Church of Santo Stefano del Cacco
Via Santo Stefano del Cacco, 26
Bus 30, 40, 62, 64, 81, 87, 492 – Largo di Torre Argentina

THE HOLY FACE OF JESUS AT SANTO STEFANO DEL CACCO

A sacred image left on the moon in 1968

On the first Tuesday of the month, at 4.30pm, a remarkable ceremony takes place in the first chapel of the left aisle of the church, during which the icon known as the Holy Face of Jesus is venerated.
Strictly speaking, this image was painted in 1945 by Gertrude Mariani (Sister Zeffirina of the Sacred Heart), based on a miraculous vision said to have been experienced by Sister Pierina De Micheli.
On 31 May 1938, in Milan, she had had a dazzling apparition of the Virgin Mary holding in her hand a medal on which the face of Christ was imprinted. The Virgin told the nun that this medal would allow whoever carried it and came each Tuesday to pray before the Holy Sacrament, to be protected against evil and enjoy the mercy of Jesus.
Jesus had already appeared to Sister Pierina De Micheli in 1932 and 1937, asking her to pray while contemplating his face.
The cult of the medal of the Holy Face was approved in August 1940 by the Archbishop of Milan and spread by, among others, Abbot Ildebrando Gregori, a Sylvestrine Benedictine monk who had been the spiritual father of Pierina De Micheli since 1940. In 1968, with the blessing of Pope Paul VI, a medal of the Holy Face was deposited on the moon by the American astronauts.
This beautiful church is commonly known as Santo Stefano del Cacco (Saint Stephen of the Monkey) because of an ancient Egyptian statue of the god Thoth represented with a dog's head, thought to be a monkey (macacco), which was found nearby (now exhibited in the Vatican Museums). The actual name of the church is Santo Stefano de Pinea: the marble pine-cone that can be seen on top of the bell tower alludes to the name of the district.
The church, which probably dates back to the 9th century, has kept its basilica form with three naves divided by two rows of columns, and in the underground crypt there are still a number of very interesting tombstones. Pope Pius IV entrusted the church to the Sylvestrine monks in 1563. Its current appearance is the result of restoration work carried out in 1607.

15.

Intersection of Via del Piè di Marmo and Via di Santo Stefano del Cacco
Bus 30, 40, 62, 64, 81, 87, 492 – Largo di Torre Argentina

THE MARBLE FOOT

A mysterious remnant of a statue at least 8 metres

Behind the Pantheon, at the intersection of Via del Piè di Marmo and Via di Santo Stefano del Cacco, stands an extraordinary sculpture: a colossal and enigmatic marble foot. Its carefully carved toes, neatly trimmed nails, the sole of the foot, and intricate leather sandal straps are all clearly visible.

The footwear appears to be a *crepida* – a type of sandal typical of ancient Greek and Roman attire – and judging by its proportions, the statue it belonged to would have been at least 8 metres tall.

It is thought, however, that the lost statue was not made entirely of marble but was probably an *acrolith*: a sculpture with marble hands, feet, and head, while the body was constructed of wood or metal and draped with fabrics.

The anonymous foot was discovered in the 16th century not far from its current location and placed on the street that now bears its name. In ancient Rome, this area of the Campo Marzio housed the grand and opulent *Iseo Campense*, an Egyptian sanctuary dedicated to the worship of Isis and Serapis. It is believed the sandal may have belonged to one of these deities.

This vast temple also housed the small obelisks that are now found in nearby Piazza della Minerva and in front of the Pantheon. Additionally, not far from the marble foot, is another relic of the area's Egyptian past: the enigmatic cat sculpture at Palazzo Grazioli (see following double page).

MOVED FOR THE FUNERAL PROCESSION TO THE PANTHEON OF ITALY'S FIRST KING

In 1878, the marble foot was relocated a few metres to its current position to make way for the funeral procession of Italy's first king en route to the Pantheon. It's said that a cobbler set up shop nearby and eagerly used the foot as a quirky advertisement for his business.

The solemn funeral was attended by the national hero Giuseppe Garibaldi, affectionately called 'Peppe' by Romans. Before the ceremony, the carriage carrying the king's coffin was paraded several times around the square so that the crowds could pay their respects. Instead of waiting at the temple's entrance with other dignitaries, Garibaldi followed the royal catafalque as it made its way around the square. This incident gave rise to the still-common Roman expression *Fare er giro de Peppe* (literally, 'to do Peppe's round'), meaning to take an unnecessarily long route.

PAOL

16.

Palazzo Grazioli
Via della Gatta
Metro B – Colosseo; Bus 30, 40, 62, 64, 81, 87, 492 – Largo di Torre Argentina

THE CAT OF PALAZZO GRAZIOLI

An ancient Egyptian feline goddess from the former Temple of Isis?

A small, discreet marble cat peers out from the string course of Palazzo Grazioli on Via della Gatta. There are various theories to explain its presence.

Some say that one night a fire broke out here, and a cat began meowing loudly, waking the residents just in time to extinguish the flames.

According to another tale, a cat's insistent cries warned a mother that her child was in imminent danger of falling from a window. Other stories claim that the cat's seemingly vacant gaze points directly to the spot where a great treasure is hidden. Others are convinced that, even after centuries, the cat marks the exact location of the hidden entrance to the lost Temple of Isis, long buried beneath the area.

In any case, it is widely believed that the small sculpture represents the ancient Egyptian cat goddess Bastet and was discovered in this neighbourhood, once home to the grand sacred area of *Iseo Campense*, the Temple of Isis on the Campo Marzio. This opulent 1st-century BCE temple was dedicated to the worship of the goddess Isis and her consort Serapis. In ancient Egyptian culture, cats were sacred creatures, symbolising fertility and the maternal protection of home and family.

The enigmatic marble foot (see previous double page), found on a nearby street, was also most likely part of this ancient place of worship.

In the concierge area at the entrance to the Palazzo Grazioli, accessible from Via del Plebiscito, is another marble cat. It has been placed there to guard the coat of arms of the Grazioli family, the building's owners since the late 19th century. During the Napoleonic era, the building served as the residence of the Austrian ambassador, and later that of Duchess Maria Luisa of Bourbon-Spain, Duchess of Lucca and formerly Queen consort of the Kingdom of Etruria, who died here in 1819.

THE VIRGIN MARY AND HER KITTEN

At the corner of Palazzo Doria Pamphilj, the 18th-century *Madonnella* on Via della Gatta depicts the Virgin Mary maternally cradling a kitten in the folds of her robe.

CURIOUS BLUE NUMBERING

Along the walls of Via della Gatta, you can still spot white ceramic tiles marked with unusual blue numbers. These are not house numbers but remnants of the locations of the old gas lamps that illuminated the city from 1854.

17.

Palazzo Mattei
Piazza Mattei, 19
Bus 30, 40, 62, 64, 81, 87, 492 – Largo di Torre Argentina

THE BOARDED-UP WINDOW AT PALAZZO MATTEI

A room with no view

There is a curious legend that Duke Mattei once lost a substantial part of his fortune. Hearing of this, his future father-in-law refused to give his daughter's hand in marriage.

So the duke decided to show the father that he had lost none of his power or nobility, and overnight had the celebrated Fountain of the Turtles built in front of the palazzo.

The palazzo was part of what was known as the Mattei district, and today its façade still forms one of the sides of the pretty square of the same name. The next day, the duke invited his beautiful fiancée and her father to his palace to put matters right. He asked them to lean out of a little window from which there was a perfect view of the sumptuous fountain and declared: 'Look what the unfortunate Duke Mattei can do in a few hours!'

The young woman's father offered his apologies and finally gave his approval to the marriage. As a souvenir of this memorable day, the duke had the window boarded up so that nobody else could appear at it. And you can still see it like that today.

The fountain was built around 1585 by the Florentine Taddeo Landini according to a design by Giacomo della Porta. It seems that on the original sketches the bronze ephebi were meant to be pushing dolphins in the upper basin, rather than the bronze turtles to which the fountain owes its name. These turtles, attributed to Bernini, were added later but have since been replaced by copies and the originals preserved in the Capitoline Museums.

WHY IS IT OFTEN WINDY IN PIAZZA DEL GESÙ?

Popular tradition holds that the square in front of the Jesuit Chiesa del Gesù is often very windy. According to a story told by Stendhal, one day the Wind, out walking with the Devil, came to the church of the Jesuits. The Devil, who had a mission to accomplish there, asked the Wind to wait for him a moment and went into the church. The Wind readily agreed, waiting one day, then two. Legend says it is still waiting there ...

18.

Piazza Giudia, Piazza delle Cinque Scole
Tram 8 – Via Arenula; Bus 30, 40, 62, 64, 81, 87, 492 – Largo di Torre Argentina

OUTLINE OF THE FORMER GHETTO FOUNTAIN

A fountain's long journey

Not until 1930, after a long journey, was the fountain designed in 1593 by the renowned Roman architect and sculptor Giacomo della Porta erected in Piazza delle Cinque Scole. Originally it stood at the heart of the vibrant Jewish ghetto, a hundred metres from its current location in Piazza Giudia. Today, a beautiful marble outline on the cobbled square marks its former position.

In 1555 Paul IV promulgated his papal bull Cum nimis absurdum, which stated that Roman Jews should not enjoy the same rights as other citizens: '… these very Jews have insolently invaded Rome … to the extent that not only have they mingled with Christians (even when close to their churches) and wearing no identifying garments, but to dwell in homes, indeed, even in the more noble … conducting business from their houses and in the streets and dealing in real estate; they even have nurses and housemaids and other Christians as hired servants'.

Jews were required to wear distinctive clothing and to live together in the same neighbourhood, the ghetto, bounded by the Tiber, the Theatre of Marcellus, the Portico of Octavia and Piazza Giudia.

In 1581, Pope Gregory XIII wanted to bring drinking water to the Campo Marzio district as well as the ghetto, but the project ground to a halt at what is now Piazza Mattei, where the nobleman Muzio Mattei was granted permission to build the so-called Fontana delle Tartarughe (Turtle Fountain, see previous double page) directly in front of his residence. In 1591, the 'Acqua Felice' at last flowed into the main square of the ghetto, Piazza Giudia.

The fountain, which was built of recycled marble from the Temple of Serapis on the Quirinal, was completed in 1593 and erected near the gallows where condemned Jews were hanged.

The upper basin, supported by a pillar, has four gorgons' heads with water flowing through their open mouths, while the main basin features the coats of arms of magistrates sitting in the year 1593.

In the 1880s the ghetto was demolished, and the whole area was reconstructed with the opening of thoroughfares such as Via Arenula, profoundly changing the earlier townscape. Pending a new location, the fountain remained in storage for many years. In 1924, the basin and pillar were reused for a fountain opposite the church of Sant'Onofrio sul Gianicolo. In 1930 the original fountain was finally reassembled on the present site.

ASTROLOGO
SOUVENIRS T-SHIRTS

19.

Palazzo Manili
Via del Portifico d'Ottavia, 1-2
Bus 8, 30, 40, 46, 62, 64, 81, 87, 492 – Largo di Torre Argentina

INSCRIPTION AT PALAZZO MANILI

Lorenzo Manili's impossible dream

Palazzo Manili is a unique complex that incorporates several Renaissance buildings. It overlooks Piazza Giudia, one of Rome's most iconic spots, where there is still a vivid sense of the city's history: the Circus Flaminius, the Theatre of Marcellus, the Portico of Octavia, the Temple of Apollo, the medieval district, the fish market, the ghetto, executions, the Nazi deportations …

In 1468, Lorenzo Manili bought several buildings, probably with the intention of joining them into one. This enterprise was not a success, due perhaps to financial difficulties, but he still wanted to leave a trace of his overwhelming love for Rome, so he covered the façades of his buildings with a long inscription in capital letters resembling those of antiquity:

URBE ROMA IN PRISTINAM FORMA(M R)ENASCENTE LAUR. MANLIUS KARITATE ERGA PATRI(AM) (A)EDIS SUO NOMINE MANLIANAS PRO FORT(UN)AR(UM) MEDIOCRITATE AD FOR(UM) IUDEOR(UM) SIBI POSTERISQ(UE) SUIS A FUND(AMENTIS) P(OSUIT). AB URB(E) CON(DITA) M.M.CCXXI L AN(NO) M(ENSE) III D(IE) II P(OSUIT) XI CAL(ENDAS) AUG(USTAS)

The text can be rendered as follows: 'At the time when the city of Rome was reborn in its ancient form, Lorenzo Manili, for love of his homeland, near the forum of the Jews, for himself and for his descendants, built up from its foundations this house, which bears the name *manliana*, at least within the limits allowed by his mediocre wealth. 2221 years after the founding of Rome, at the age of 50 years, 3 months and 2 days, he built this house on the eleventh day before the beginning of August'.

Manili also affixed fragments of reliefs to the façades. On some of the windows to the left of the complex, those overlooking Piazza Costaguti, he had carved the motto 'HAVE ROMA' (Take care, Rome).

Manili's initiative – bizarre as it may seem – is important because it demonstrates better than any book the cultural climate in Rome during the flowering of humanism, when the language, literature, history and values of the classical world were being rediscovered.

It was a world that must have seemed like a sort of golden age to Manili's contemporaries.

Had it been within his means, Manili might have built a new Colosseum. Nevertheless, he left this memorable inscription, witness to a wonderful and impossible dream.

VRBE·ROMA·INPRISTINAM·FOR
NOMINE·MANLIAN AS·PRO·FOR
LAVR·MANLIVS·FVNDAVIT
LAVR·MANLIVS·AE

THE VATICAN AND SURROUNDING

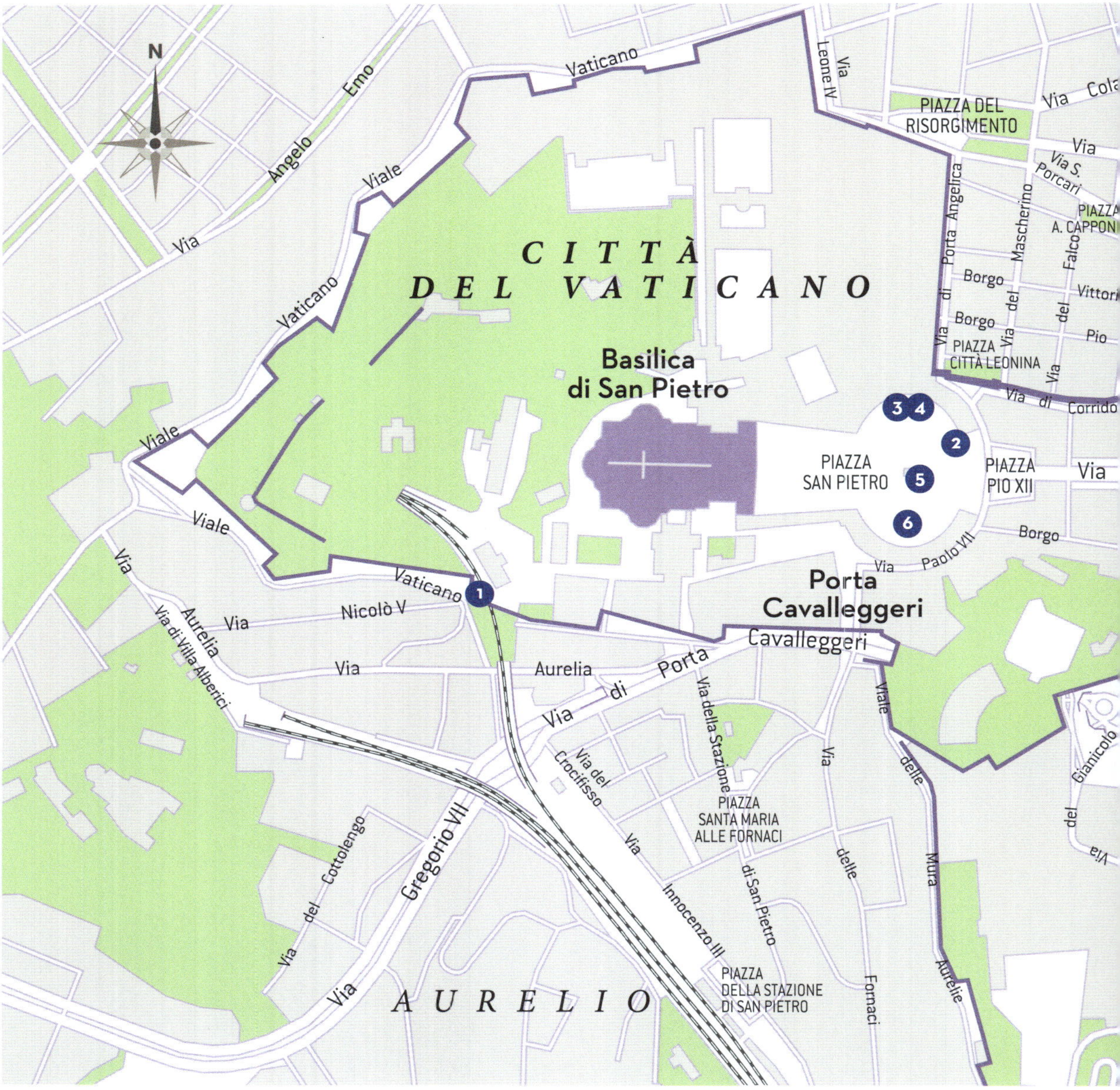

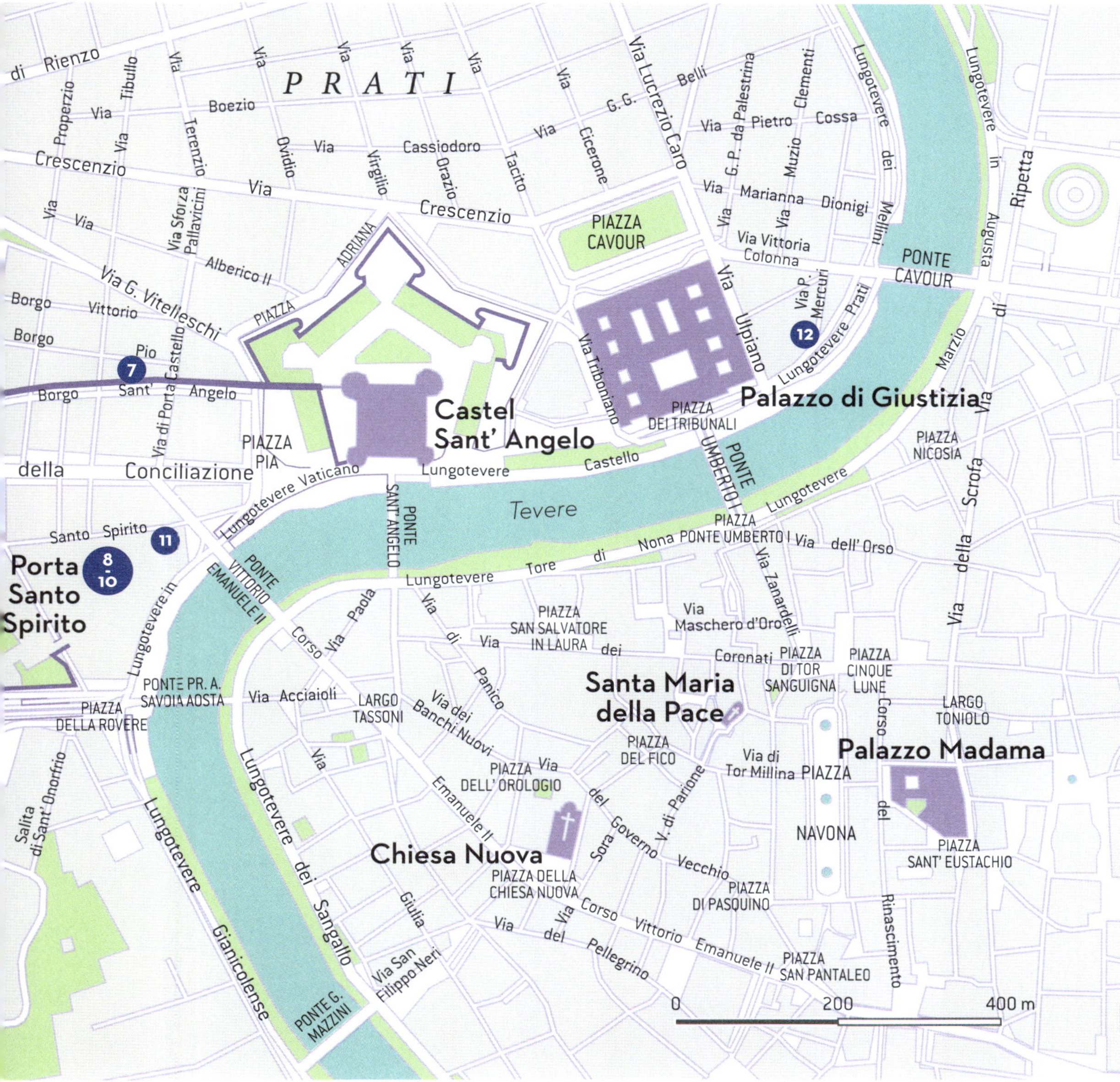

07. PASSETTO ARCHES *p. 134*

08. NATIONAL MUSEUM OF THE HISTORY OF MEDICINE *p. 136*

09. MONUMENTAL COMPLEX OF SANTO SPIRITO IN SASSIA *p. 138*

10. THE ITALIAN CLOCK OF THE PALAZZO DEL COMMENDATORE *p. 140*

11. THE FOUNDLINGS' WHEEL *p. 142*

12. MUSEUM OF THE SOULS IN PURGATORY *p. 144*

01.

Via della Stazione Vaticana
Bus 34, 36 – Aurelia/Bonifacio VIII

THE POPE'S RAILWAY

The shortest international railway in the world

1270 metres – this is the total length of the Vatican railway built (following the Lateran Treaty of 11 February 1929) to link the Holy See with the Italian rail network via a junction with the nearby station of Roma San Pietro.

Construction work was finished in 1932. It involved erecting the 143-metre-long Gelsomino ('Jasmine') viaduct, built of masonry faced with travertine and brick. The track passes under a wide arch surmounted by the coat of arms of Pope Pius XI and goes through the Leonine Wall to enter the State of the Vatican City.

A majestic sliding double gate – weighing over 35 tonnes – closes this passage, which is only open on rare occasions to allow a freight convoy through.

A short distance beyond the gate is Vatican City station, opened in 1933 and now a shopping centre.

The track continues for another hundred metres or so to end in a cul-de-sac: an 80-metre-long tunnel, with two parallel sidings used for shunting.

During the preparations for Jubilee 2000 at Roma San Pietro station, one of two tracks along the viaduct was taken up, to be replaced by a pleasant walkway with a fine view of the gate and an unusual perspective on *Er Cuppolone*, the immense dome of Saint Peter's.

02.

Largo del Colonnato
Metro A – Ottaviano

SYMBOLISM OF THE FONTANELLA DELLE TRE TIARE

Triple tiara for a threefold symbol

The Fountain of the Three Tiaras, designed by the Roman architect Pietro Lombardi in 1927, stands on a raised circular plinth divided into three, in the centre of which are three basins into which the water flows. The whole structure is surmounted by three papal tiaras arranged in a triangle. Under each is a set of pontifical keys.

These three tiaras represent the triple crown (*triregnum*), the papal crown shaped like a beehive that is placed on the pope's head during the coronation ceremony to mark the beginning of a pontificate. Popes can either wear the tiara of their predecessors or have a new one made. It is a non-liturgical ornament (the pope, like the bishops, wears a papal mitre for acts of worship) that is only used for papal processions and solemn acts of jurisdiction.

The first mention of the use of the triple crown goes back to the 8th century, although its ornamentation and shape kept evolving until the mid-14th century.

The last pope to wear the triregnum regularly was Paul VI in 1963. Since then popes have rarely worn it, although with its crossed keys attached by a cord it remains a potent symbol of the papacy.

The origins of the papal tiara go back to Pope Sylvester I (314–335), who had received the crown of the Emperor Constantine as a sign of freedom and peace in the Church, the beginning of the Pax Romana.

According to another source, it was Clovis I who gave the papal crown to Pope Symmachus in the church of Saint Martin of Tours, France, in the 5th century.

The lowest of the three tiers of the triple crown appeared at the base of the traditional white hat worn by popes in the 9th century, when they took on the temporal power of the Papal States.

This crown was decorated with jewels to resemble those of kings and princes. The term 'tiara' is mentioned for the first time in 1118, in the biography of Pope Paschal II, *Liber Pontificalis*.

A second tier was added to the first in 1301, during the pontificate of Boniface VIII at a time of conflict with Philip IV ('the Fair') of France, in order to demonstrate his spiritual authority over the royal power, and the crown was renamed the *biregnum*.

When the third tier was added – apparently during the reign of John XXII (1316–1334) – the crown took the name *triregnum*.

The three tiers were given the following papal attributes derived from the triple dimensions of Christ – priest, prophet and king: universal pastor (upper crown), supremacy of spiritual authority (middle crown) and domination of temporal power (lower crown), but also emperor of bodies, souls and minds, enjoying absolute sovereignty over Hell, Earth and Heaven.

The pontifical cord connects the three worlds to which the keys give access.

© Galzu

WHY ARE THE KEYS A PAPAL SYMBOL?

It was Jesus Christ himself who conferred on Saint Peter, the first pope, the authority of the supreme head of the Church in the Gospel according to Saint Matthew (16:19): 'And I will give unto thee the keys of the kingdom of heaven.' There are two keys: one gold (heavenly), the other silver (terrestrial), which symbolise the ability to open and close the gates of Paradise.

03.

Piazza San Pietro
Metro A – Ottaviano

THE WHITE MARBLE DISCS OF ST. PETER'S SQUARE

The optical illusion of St. Peter's Square

The construction of St. Peter's Square was commissioned by Pope Alexander VII to Bernini, who was immediately appointed as the official architect. The main function of this space was to contain the crowds that gathered here for the *Urbi et Orbi* Papal Blessing that was given on Easter Sunday from the central balcony (called the Loggia of the Blessings). But the layout of the square also had to take into account that much smaller crowds also gathered here for the weekly Sunday Blessing given by the pope from a window of his Vatican apartment on the right side of the square. Bernini kept the trapezoidal shape of the existing square in front of the church, which was mainly designed according to the existing buildings, and created a large elliptical square bordered by two semi-circular colonnades, each consisting of four rows of columns. With this layout, Bernini wanted to symbolise the outstretched arms of the church embracing its flock. Bernini's plan was both symbolic and aesthetic. The façade of St. Peter's Basilica that was built by Maderno (flanked at the time by the foundations of two towers that were later demolished) was too large and too low. Bernini attempted to rectify the imbalance by using optical illusions: the low-lying colonnades make the façade appear taller, while the width of the square counterbalances the width of the façade. At the centre of the ellipse stands an obelisk. On its right, a fountain designed by Maderno was built on the main axis and the foci of the ellipse. Bernini built and installed another identical fountain on the other side. Both fountains are equidistant from the colonnades and the obelisk. This is where the most striking optical illusion is found: on the main axis, between the fountains and the obelisk, is a white marble disc marking the centre of the virtual circle formed by the colonnades. Seen from this marble disc, the four rows of columns symbolising the arms of the church perfectly align with each other, appearing as one.

CENTRO DEL COLONNATO

04.

Piazza San Pietro
Metro A – Ottaviano

THE PLAQUE DESIGNATING THE ORIGINAL LOCATION OF THE OBELISK ON ST. PETER'S SQUARE

Le centre de l'ancien cirque de Caligula

Another plaque located between the Basilica and the Teutonic Cemetery on Piazza dei Protomartiri Cristiani serves as a reminder of the obelisk now located on St. Peter's Square, which was used to mark the central spina of Caligula's circus. Pope Sixtus V decided to move the obelisk to St. Peter's Square, provoking a legendary incident in the process.

The task involved lifting the 320-tonne obelisk and moving it 300 metres in order to erect it at the centre of the square. Domenico Fontana was chosen by the pope to command the operation, which required the efforts of 160 horses and 900 men. The men were given the order to march to the sound of the trumpet and stop to the sound of the bell. Any noise likely to interfere with the transmission of orders would be punishable by death, but as the ropes began to fray, a man shouted from the crowd, 'Acqua alle funi!' ('Water to the ropes!'). Water was thrown on the ropes, causing them to retract, and the disaster was averted. Benedetto Bresca, the sea captain who dared to shout out, was exempted from the death penalty. After Bernini finished redesigning the square in 1660, a plaque commemorating the location where the obelisk was erected on 10 September 1586 was placed about four metres from its actual location, at the exact centre of St Peter's Basilica's façade.

The assassination attempt of Pope John Paul II on 13 May 1981 took place on the right side of St. Peter's Square. The spot is marked by a small square plaque of white marble bearing the date of the tragedy in Roman numerals and the coat of arms of John Paul II.

CIRCI FLAMINII SPECIM: EN SVO CVM EVRIPO
ARIS QVE ET SIMVLAC HRO ISIDIS LEONE IN:
SIDENTIS OPERA ET ST VDIO PYRRHI LIGORI:
PICTORIS NEAPOLITANI A: NTIQVARII ACCVRATISSIM
ET SOLERTISSIMI IAM PRIDE: M EX VETVSTIS MONVMEN:
TIS EDVCTVM. FIDELISSIME N: VNC DENVO CLAVDIVS DVCH:
ETVS ÆNEIS TABELLIS EXCVLPT: VM IN LVCEM PRODIRE CVRAVIT.
M.D.L XXXI.
OBELISCVS SOLI SACER
EVRIPVS
HIPPODROMVS
APOLLINI
LVNA
META CVM SVIS OVIS
META CVM SVIS OVIS
BIGAE
EQVO SINGVLARI
BIGAE
EQVO SING
CARCERES XII

SITO DELL
OBELISCO VATICANO
FINO ALL'ANNO
MDLXXXVI

© Sailko

05.

Piazza San Pietro
Metro A – Ottaviano

SAINT PETER'S MERIDIAN

A forgotten giant sundial

Since 1817, the famous obelisk of Saint Peter's Square – a red granite monolith over 25 metres high, or 40 metres if you count the base and the cross – is one of the world's largest gnomons marking a meridian (see the Place de la Concorde meridian in *Paris – The Secret Atlas*, in this series of books).

On the paving stones of the square is a strip of granite that forms a straight line linking a point to the right of the base of the obelisk to another point beyond the Maderno fountain.

At each end of this strip, two marble discs indicate the points where, at midday, the shadow of the cross is projected during the summer solstice (in the sign of Cancer) and the winter solstice (in the sign of Capricorn). Five more discs mark the passage of the sun through the other signs of the zodiac, arranged in pairs: Leo-Gemini, Virgo-Taurus, Libra-Aries, Scorpio-Pisces and Sagittarius-Aquarius.

The obelisk was probably erected at Heliopolis during the 12th dynasty (20th–18th centuries BCE). Caligula had it brought to Rome in 37 CE to set off his private circus, on the Vatican hill, before it was taken over by Nero. Several popes have attempted to embellish or otherwise make their mark on the obelisk. Sixtus V, for example, decided to add four lions to the base as a reference to the coat of arms of his family, the Peretti, and he donated the bronze ball that surmounts the obelisk, claimed to contain the ashes of Caesar, to the municipality of Rome. Alexander VII crowned it with the Chigi symbols of mountains and stars, and Innocent XIII added the bronze eagles and the heraldic emblems of the Conti family.

TORO 21 APRILE ✶ VERGINE 23 AGOSTO

06.

Quadrante del Libeccio
Piazza San Pietro
Metro A – Ottaviano

NERONE'S HEART OF STONE

A mysterious stone

Amid the seemingly identical volcanic cobblestones of St Peter's Square lies one that stands out due to its enigmatic heart shape. Located a few metres from the great obelisk, near the marble disc marking the southwest wind (*Libeccio*), this peculiar *sampietrino* (cobblestone) has sparked countless stories and legends.

It is said that local children from the Borgo district stumbled upon it during their games and nicknamed it 'Nero's Heart'. The stone became a source of mystery and fascination. According to one legend, the heart-shaped stone silently commemorates the Christian martyrs executed in Nero's Circus, which once stood on this very site. Another tale claims it was embedded in the pavement by a widow protesting the unjust execution of her husband by the Pope.

Other stories weave a more romantic narrative: some say the heart was carved by Michelangelo as a tribute to a lost love, while others attribute it to Gian Lorenzo Bernini, the designer of the square, reflecting his melancholy over never finding his soulmate.

Some have interpreted the shape as resembling the ace of spades, speculating it was etched under cover of night by an anonymous fortune-teller. Others trace its origin to pivotal moments in Rome's history. For instance, a tale recounts that on 2 July 1849, as Giuseppe Garibaldi assembled the soldiers of the Roman Republic in the square following their surrender to French forces, a young soldier left the heart as a symbolic farewell to the city. Another story claims that the stone was placed here in September 1870 by a bored Papal Zouave waiting for orders during the Piedmontese siege at Porta Pia.

A more scientific theory links the stone to Filippo Luigi Gilij (1756–1821), an astronomer and naturalist who, in 1817, designed the square's meridian sundial and the *Rosa dei Venti* around the obelisk. If viewed as an inverted heart, the shape may represent the outline of a South American pear tomato (*Solanum lycopersicum pyriforme*), a plant the abbot cultivated in the Vatican and described in his 1789 botanical work *Observazioni fitologiche sopra alcune piante esotiche introdotte in Roma* (Phytological observations on some exotic plants introduced in Rome).

Alternatively, the heart-shaped cobblestone might be a fragment of an ancient Roman inscription or, more likely, an ornamental motif from a red porphyry basin similar to the one forming the main altar of the Basilica of San Bartolomeo all'Isola on Tiber Island.

THE *SAMPIETRINO*

St Peter's Square lends its name to the iconic *sampietrini*, the volcanic cobblestones paving much of Rome's historic districts. First introduced in 1725 during the square's repaving, they solved a pressing issue: the Pope's carriage had nearly overturned due to uneven ground, prompting the need for a sturdier surface.

07.

Borgo Sant'Angelo
Bus 23 – Via della Traspontina

PASSETTO ARCHES

Vestiges of a truly extraordinary project

Along the street known as Borgo Sant'Angelo, behind the church of Santa Maria in Traspontina, the wall of Il Passetto is pierced by three arches bearing the arms of Pope Clement VIII (1592–1605). These openings, which today connect the districts of Borgo Sant'Angelo and Borgo Pio, look quite ordinary and yet they owe their existence to a truly extraordinary project, instigated by none other than Julius Caesar.

The history of Rome may be said to have begun in the 10th century BCE, thanks to a shallow stretch of the river at the Isola Tiberina (Tiber Island), where easy access to both banks encouraged trade. Winter floods, however, often brought destruction and devastation to the city.

Julius Caesar recognised that the problem was caused by too many bends in the river as it ran through the city, so his solution was to 'correct' its course. He planned a perfectly straight new riverbed that would leave the original course at Monte Mario to rejoin it at Trastevere.

In imperial Rome, the river was properly maintained by a designated authority whose exclusive duties were to look after the river. In the Middle Ages, however, the strengthening of the ancient Roman bridges formed an additional barrier to the flow of water.

Then on 25 December 1598, a flood of unprecedented magnitude led to disaster in the city: the Tiber rose almost 20 metres. So Caesar's original project was resurrected by Clement VIII, who decided in 1599 to have a new riverbed dug: the river at Monte Mario was to be channelled into a 'ditch' as far as Santo Spirito hospital, where it was supposed to meet up with the old course. The only obstacle was the Passetto di Borgo, which is why Clement VIII had three arches opened in the wall.

However, the project remained dead in the water because the pope's advisers, worried about the proximity of the river and the newly built church of Santa Maria in Traspontina, suggested diverting the water into Castel Sant'Angelo's moat, so that it would flow directly into the original riverbed. That project met with no success either. The solution was only found after yet another destructive flood (1870), with the construction of the Lungotevere (riverside quays) and the realisation of a dream.

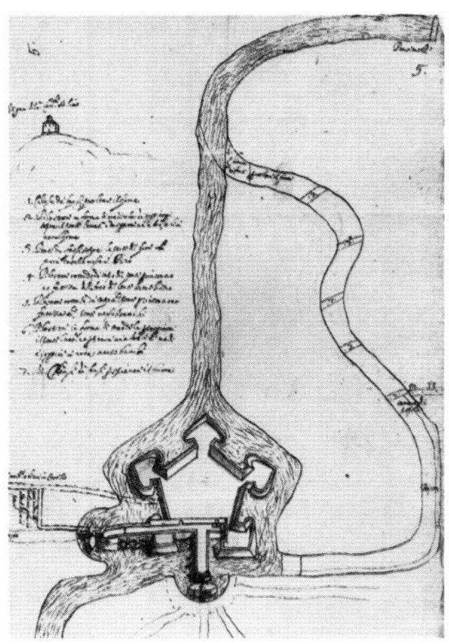

PARCOMETRO

08.

Lungotevere in Sassia, 3
Bus 23 – Piazza della Rovere

NATIONAL MUSEUM OF THE HISTORY OF MEDICINE

A little museum of horrors

The museum, which was planned after the First World War to bring together medical material collected for the 1911 World Fair, was opened in 1933 in nine large rooms at the Pio Istituto di Santo Spirito (Pious Institute of the Holy Spirit). There is no other museum in Italy with as many artefacts relating to the history of medicine as this one. The visit starts in the Sala Alessandrina on the ground floor, with hand-painted anatomical tables from the 17th and 18th centuries hanging on the walls.

The Sala Flaiani contains the remains of one of the most important anatomical museums of Europe, the Museo di Santo Spirito (Museum of the Holy Spirit), founded in the 18th century by the great surgeon Flaiani. Here one can observe several anatomical preparations that have been kept unaltered over the centuries thanks to refined preservation techniques. These include skeletal alterations, examples of pathological anatomy, deformed foetuses, skulls and limbs affected by syphilis and mummified heads. In the centre of the room there is a mill in the form of a wooden temple, which was used to grind quinine.

The next hall is the Sala Capparoni, where a series of incredibly realistic Roman and Etruscan ex voto offerings are preserved along with other modern wax ex voto offerings, as well as a collection of Roman, medieval, Renaissance and 19th-century surgical instruments, and a phial of scorpion oil for poisonous animal bites and stings. There are also some snakes' tongues, a crown used for headaches, Renaissance first-aid kits, a collection of glass and ceramic receptacles used to keep medicines and a 19th-century electrotherapy machine. The Sala Carbonelli today houses fascinating and macabre objects and instruments: a collection of drills, saws for amputations from the 16th to the 19th centuries, anal and vaginal specula from the 15th to the 19th centuries, microscopes and glasses of all shapes and from all periods, the two glass beakers used by Avogadro to demonstrate the law of the compression of gases, a girl's hand metallised by a process that is still unknown, a huge wooden 17th-century press for extracting plant essences, and some stone and metal mortars for making medicinal potions. The reconstructions of an old pharmacy and the chemical-alchemical laboratory from the 17th century are beautiful. You can also admire a 16th-century walnut bookcase with over 10,000 books, prints and reviews concerning the history of medicine on its shelves.

09.

Borgo San Spirito, 1-2-3
Bus 23 – Piazza della Rovere

MONUMENTAL COMPLEX OF SANTO SPIRITO IN SASSIA

Rare visit to a former hospital

Once a week, the remarkable architectural ensemble of Santo Spirito in Sassia is open to visitors.

On the initiative of the King of Wessex, the 'Schola Saxonum' (Saxon School), a charitable institution for Saxon pilgrims on their way to visit Saint Peter's tomb in Rome, was created in the 8th century. The buildings, later destroyed by fire and pillaging, were reconstructed at the end of the 12th century on the orders of Pope Innocent III, who dedicated the main section to helping the sick, paupers and abandoned babies.

Under the name Santo Spirito in Sassia, it grew into the most advanced hospital of its time. The grand rectangular gallery could receive up to a thousand people. The tour begins in the Corsia Sistina (Sistine Ward), which Pope Sixtus IV added to the hospital two centuries later. The gallery, 120 metres in length and 13 metres high, is divided into two sections by a majestic tiburium, in the centre of which rises a very beautiful altar, the only work by Palladio to be found in Rome. The interior portal, finely carved in marble and attributed to Andrea Bregno, is called the Portale del Paradiso (Heaven's Door). Next to this entrance is the 'foundlings' wheel (see page 142).

Sixtus IV had the walls of this gallery frescoed to the level of the windows to celebrate the establishment of the hospital and the merits of Innocent III, as well as for his own glory. He also ordered the construction of two buildings adjoining the superb cloisters, reserved respectively for the monks and nuns who worked at the institute (at present, only the priest's quarters are open to the public).

Around 1570, Monseigneur Cirillo, then Commander of the brotherhood, enlarged the hospital by building the Palazzo del Commendatore around a splendid courtyard. A grand staircase leads to the upper gallery where frescoes by Ercole Perillo entirely cover the upper part of the walls.

This gallery leads into the Lancisiana library (18th century, currently under restoration), and the Commander's former apartment, decorated with sculptures, tapestries, antique furniture and frescoes by Jacopo and Francesco Zucchi telling the story of the hospital.

10.

Former hospital of Santo Spirito in Sassia
Borgo San Spirito, 1-2-3
Bus 23 – Piazza della Rovere

THE ITALIAN CLOCK OF THE PALAZZO DEL COMMENDATORE

A clock with only six hours

A huge and unusual clock dominates the courtyard of the former Santo Spirito architectural ensemble, set in the cornice of the Palazzo del Commendatore (Palace of the Commander, as the president of the charitable institution of Santo Spirito used to be known).

This curious Baroque clock dates back to 1828 and has the particularity of possessing an 'Italian' face, divided into six sections (see below). The clock face is encircled by a serpent biting its own tail, while a bronze lizard (symbol of death and resurrection) takes the place of a hand.

WHAT IS THE ORIGIN OF 'ITALIAN' CLOCKS?

The subdivision of the day into hours goes back to antiquity and was probably introduced by the Chaldeans. Whereas the Babylonians and Chinese measured time in double hours, 12 kaspars a day for the former and 12 tokis for the latter, the Greeks and Romans divided the day into two equal parts of 12 hours each. As the time from sunrise to sunset varied with the season, daylight hours in summer were longer than the hours of darkness, while the reverse held true in winter. The rigorous discipline of monastic orders, especially the Benedictines, led to a radical upheaval in ways of measuring time. The hour began to be calculated by sundials that did not show the hour, but the religious duty to be fulfilled at various moments of day and night (matins, vespers, etc.). At the end of the 13th century, mechanical clocks made their appearance in Europe. This was a true revolution, as from then on the hour had a fixed duration, to such an extent that by the end of the 14th century most towns had abandoned the solar hour indicated by a gnomon to organise themselves by the striking of the church tower clock. The day began at sunset and was divided into 24 hours: consequently the clock faces were graduated from I to XXIV. However, people soon got tired of counting 24 chimes, not to mention the innumerable errors that occurred. So from the 15th century the system was modified so that the clock would strike only six times a day instead of 24. Little time was wasted in applying this simplification and so clock faces began to be numbered I to VI, like that of San Niccolò Castle. During the Napoleonic campaigns, 'Italian' time was replaced by 'French-style' time, where clocks were numbered I to XII and the day started at midnight.

VI

11.

Former hospital of Santo Spirito in Sassia
Borgo San Spirito, 1-2-3
Bus 23 – Piazza della Rovere

THE FOUNDLINGS' WHEEL

For abandoning your child discreetly

Backing onto the right-hand side of the Santo Spirito in Sassia complex, you can still see today a small construction fitted with a grille through which can be glimpsed a 'foundlings' wheel intended to discreetly receive unwanted newborn infants (see below).
Before these wheels existed, the most common practice was 'oblation' (offering to God), which was not considered abandonment since the parents 'gave' their child to a convent that not only welcomed it but offered it a place in monastic life. In Italy, the first wheel was installed at this hospital by Pope Innocent III in 1198. In the second half of the 19th century there were 1,200 'wheels' of this kind in Italy, but they were abolished from 1867 and finally disappeared in 1923.

WHAT IS A FOUNDLINGS' WHEEL?

It is said that in 787, Dateus, a priest in Milan, began placing a large basket outside his church so that abandoned infants could be left there.
More organised initiatives for the reception of abandoned children were begun by the Hospice des Chanoines in Marseille from 1188 onwards, with Pope Innocent III (1198–1216) later giving the practice the Church's benediction; he had been horrified by the terrible sight of the bodies of abandoned infants floating in the Tiber and was determined to do something to save them.
So the doors of convents were equipped with a sort of rotating cradle which made it possible for parents to leave their infant anonymously and without exposing it to the elements.
The infant was left in the outside section of the cradle, and then the parent rang a bell so that the nuns could activate the mechanism and bring the child inside. Access to the 'turntable' was, however, protected by a grille so narrow that only newborn infants would fit through.
Abandoned during the 19th century, the system had to be readopted after some twenty years at various places in Europe due to the sharp upturn in the number of infants abandoned.
You can see historic foundling wheels at the Vatican, Pisa and Florence (see the *Secret Tuscany* guide from the same publisher), in Bayonne and in Barcelona (see the *Secret Barcelona* guide).

12.

Church of the Sacro Cuore del Suffragio
Lungotevere Prati, 12
Bus 30, 70, 81, 87, 100, 280, 492 – Piazza Cavour

MUSEUM OF THE SOULS IN PURGATORY

Traces of the netherworld

The church of the Sacro Cuore del Suffragio (Sacred Heart of Suffrage) was built at the behest of Father Victor Jouet, a French priest from Marseille, who acquired a large plot of building land in Lungotevere Prati in 1893. The peculiarity of this building, which was designed by Giuseppe Gualandi, is that it is entirely built in Gothic style, so much so that some have called it the 'small dome of Milan'.

In 1897 a fire broke out in a chapel that no longer exists, dedicated to Our Lady of the Rosary, and when the fire was extinguished, faithful bystanders noticed that on one side of the altar there was the image of a face, which, it was said, belonged to a soul in Purgatory. This amazing event prompted Father Jouet to try to find other testimonies concerning the souls in Purgatory. The result of his research is the collection that is preserved today in a showcase hanging on the wall of a small corridor leading to the sacristy.

The collection consists of about a dozen disturbing relics in the form of writing material, fabrics, books and photos that testify to presumed contact between the living and souls in Purgatory. These signs have been left by the souls of the deceased asking for prayers and indulgence.

The relics found here are quite enigmatic: the imprint of three fingers left in 1871 on Maria Zaganti's book of devotion by the deceased Palmira Rastelli who was asking for a holy mass to be said for her; the photo of an imprint by the deceased Mrs Leleux burned into the sleeve of her son Giuseppe's shirt during her apparition in 1789 in Wodecq in Belgium; the burned imprint of Sister Maria di San Luigi Gonzaga's finger when she appeared to Sister Maria of the Sacred Heart in 1894; and finally the imprint left on Margherita Demmerle's book by her mother-in-law who appeared 30 years after her death, in the parish of Ellinghen in 1815.

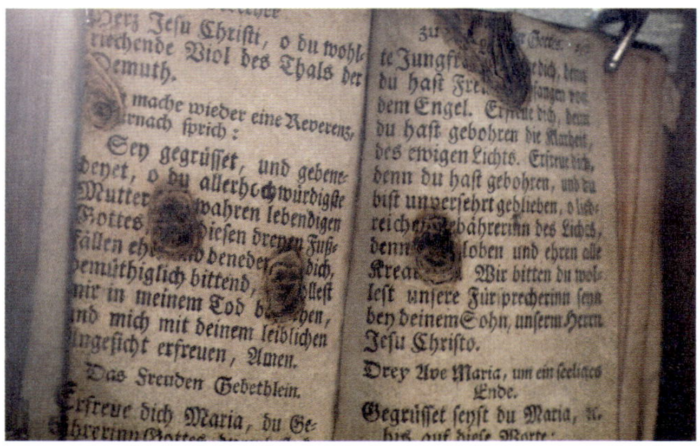

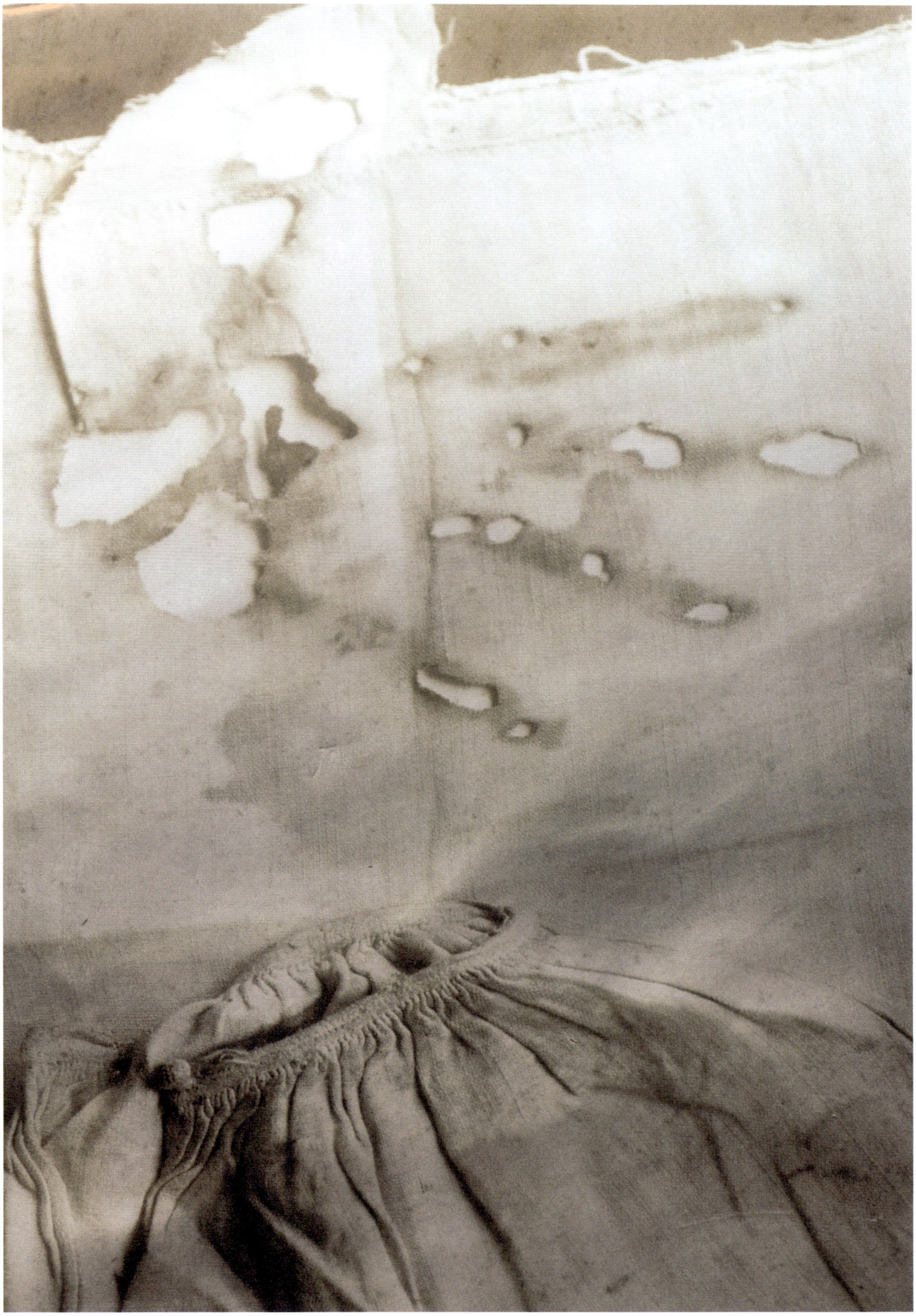

N
GIANICOLO
AURELIO
TRASTEVERE
Tevere
Parco
Gianicolense
Orto
Botanico
Villa
Aurelia
Villa
Sciarra
Villa
Farnesina
Porta Settimiana
Santa Maria della Scala
Fontana dell'
Acqua Paola
San Pietro in Montorio
Porta San Pancrazio
PIAZZA
DELLA ROVERE
PONTE PR.
A. SAVOIA AOSTA
PIAZZA DI
SANT' ONOFRIO
PIAZZA
DEL FARO
PIAZZA G.
GARIBALDI
PIAZZALE
AURELIO
LARGO
TRE GIUGNO 1849
PONTE G.
MAZZINI
Corso Vittorio
Via dei Banchi Vecchi
Via Giulia
Vicolo del Cefalo
Via del Gonfalone
Via San Filippo Neri
Via dei Sangallo
Lungotevere
Lungotevere dei Tebaldi
Lungotevere della Farnesina
Via della Lungara
Via della Lungara
Via Gianicolo
Salita di Sant' Onofrio
Via del Gianicolo
Via della Gianicolense
Via degli Orti d'Alibert
Via delle Mantellate
Via di San Francesco di Salles
Via della Penitenza
Via dei Riari
Via Corsini
Via Garibaldi
Via della Scala
Via dei Mattonato
Via dei Panieri
Via di Porta San Pancrazio
Via Angelo Masina
Via Giacomo Medici
Via Trenta Aprile
Via Fabrizi
Viale Glorioso
Via Goffredo Mameli
Via Nicola Fabrizi
Via Calandrelli
Via Dandolo
Via Filippo Casini
Via Dandolo
Viale delle Mura Aurelie
Via delle Fornaci
Via Nuova delle Fornaci
Via di San Pancrazio
Via Aurelia Antica
Passeggiata del Gianicolo
Viale delle Mura Gianicolensi
Via Giacinto Carini
Via del Vascello
Via A. Algardi
Via Fratelli Bonnet
Via Basilio Bricci
Via dei Quattro Venti
Via Fr. Bolognesi
Via Oreste Regnoli
0
100
200 m
1
2
3
4
7

GIANICOLO

01.

Outside wall of the church of San Pietro in Montorio
Via Garibaldi
Bus 115 – Garibaldi/Iacobucci

SAN PIETRO IN MONTORIO'S CANNON BALL

An unusual souvenir of the fighting on Janiculum Hill in 1849

If you look to the left on the façade of the church of San Pietro in Montorio, you will see a strange plaque with a sphere attached to it. Step closer to read the inscription and you will discover a French artillery cannon ball found at this very spot. It commemorates the 1849 battles during which the independent republic of Rome put up a heroic defence.
1849 was a decisive year for the Risorgimento, the ideological and political movement behind Italian unification. In Rome, papal rule foundered in the face of popular pro-democracy uprisings, and the pope was obliged to flee the city. The republic was proclaimed on 9 February. The conservative European regimes offered help to restore temporal power while Garibaldi and his followers disembarked at Rome to defend the new republic. He was entrusted with the defence of Janiculum Hill, the point most exposed to the French army offensive.

GARIBALDI: SAVIOUR OF TASSO'S BELL

It was in 1595 that the smallest bell of the church of Sant'Onofrio al Gianicolo had come to be known as 'Tasso's bell'. On 25 April of that year, its melancholy peals accompanied the death throes and announced the end – at the age of only 51 – of the celebrated poet who was being cared for in the neighbouring convent.
In spring 1849, this bell was almost destroyed during the rioting that gripped the capital. The order had gone out to confiscate all church bells to make cannons, and as it was not far from the fighting Sant'Onofrio was one of the first churches to be requisitioned by the military.
The story goes that the Father Superior vainly begged the officer in charge to take whatever he liked except the little bell, but he would not be moved, until Garibaldi arrived in the nick of time. As a last resort, the priest appealed directly to the general.
Moved by his supplications, or perhaps by the sad early death of a great poet, Garibaldi ordered that Tasso's bell be spared.
Thus it can still be seen today, as well as the tomb and the convent cell where the unfortunate author of the immortal Gerusalemme liberata died.

MINISTERO PER I BENI CULTURALI E AMBIENTALI
SOPRINTENDENZA PER I BENI AMBIENTALI ED ARCHITETTONICI DI ROMA
PROIETTILE DI CANNONE DA 140
DELL'ARTIGLIERIA FRANCESE
- MEMORIA BELLICA
DEI BOMBARDAMENTI
DEL GIUGNO 1849 -
QUI' TROVATO E RIPOSTO
IN RICORDO
DELL'EROICA RESISTENZA DELLA REPUBBLICA ROMANA
E DEI GRAVI DANNI ALLORA SOFFERTI
DA QUESTA INSIGNE CAPPELLA
- ORA NUOVAMENTE RESTAURATA -
OPERA DI CARLO MADERNO
A. D. MDCCCCXCV

02.

Via Angelo Masina, 5
Bus 115, 870 – Mura Gianicolensi

AMERICAN ACADEMY IN ROME

Artists' workshops inspired by the pavilions of the 1893 Chicago World's Fair

The American Academy, even more discreet than other similar Roman institutions, accepts some 30 artists and researchers per year, as well as around forty short-stay students. The project to set up an American Academy in Rome emerged following the Chicago Columbian Exposition of 1893 and was based on the idea of a group led by two architects: Charles Follen McKim, who designed some of the buildings of Columbia University (1893) and the Pierpont Morgan Library (1903) in New York; and Daniel Burnham, responsible for the Flatiron Building in New York (1902). These men attached great significance to European classical culture, and would convince the biggest New York financiers of the time (J.P. Morgan, John D. Rockefeller and Henry Clay Frick) to make substantial donations to establish the American Academy in Rome in 1894.

Today, the artists' workshops in front of the outer façade are reminiscent of the pavilions of the 1893 Chicago Exposition, while the academy's main building, designed by McKim, Mead and White, was inspired by Renaissance villas with a piano nobile (main floor) and a courtyard ornamented with the remains of antique sculptures.

The beautiful Villa Aurelia was built for Cardinal Girolamo Farnese in 1650. In 1849, Garibaldi set up his headquarters there to defend the Roman Republic against the French armies, whose artillery almost destroyed the villa and its gardens in their victorious battle. After major restoration work, the villa was bequeathed to the American Academy in 1909. Conferences and concerts are regularly held there.

In the gardens, the Casa Rustica stands on the site of the 16th-century casino of Cardinal Malvasia. On 14 April 1611, the Accademia dei Lincei held a grand reception there in honour of Galileo, whose guests could view the heavens through the telescope he had invented. The casino was demolished in 1849 and replaced by the Casa Rustica, which houses maps produced by NASA representing the sky on 14 April 1611. The building was used as a tavern until the 1920s (the inscription 'VINO' can still be seen), when it was bought by the Academy.

03.

Passeggiata del Gianicolo
Bus 115, 870 – Piazzale Garibaldi G.

THE FAÇADE OF 'MICHELANGELO'S HOUSE'

A façade that was moved three times

While strolling along the Passeggiata del Gianicolo (Janiculum Walk), just opposite the statue of Ciceruacchio ('the chubby one', the nickname of Angelo Brunetti) you will come across a beautiful 16th-century façade with a plaque bearing this inscription: QUESTA FACCIATA DELLA CASA DETTA DI MICHELANGELO GIÀ IN VIA DELLE TRE PILE DEMOLITA NELL'ANNO MCMXXX FU RICOSTRUITA AD ORNAMENTO DELLA PASSEGGIATA PUBBLICA XXI APRILE MCMXLI.*

What was said to be 'Michelangelo's house' stood near the first bend in Via delle Tre Pile, the lane that climbs up to the right of the Cordonata (flight of steps designed by Michelangelo leading to Piazza d'Aracoeli) on the Capitoline Hill. In 1872 the building was demolished, but the architectural elements of the façade were purchased by the architect Domenico Jannetti, who recycled them in a new construction in Via delle Tre Pile. Then, during the 1930s construction work on the Capitoline Hill, Jannetti's building was in turn demolished, but once again the 16th-century façade was preserved. It was dismantled and stored in a municipal depot, only to be reused in 1941 to conceal a large water tank at the end of the Passeggiata del Gianicolo from the gaze of the Romans.

It is extraordinary that this façade has been attributed to Michelangelo's house: he lived elsewhere, in the Macel de' Corvi district, as borne out by the inscription at the junction of Piazza Venezia and Via dei Fornari which translates as: 'On this site stood the house consecrated by the occupancy and death of the divine Michelangelo.'

Michelangelo did indeed live in Macel de' Corvi until his death on 18 February 1564. The house was then bought by Daniele da Volterra, one of his pupils, nicknamed *braghettone* ('breeches-maker') because at the height of the Counter-Reformation he was responsible for covering up the nudity of several figures (painted by his master) in the Sistine Chapel's Last Judgment fresco.

Between the late 19th and early 20th centuries, the south and east sides of Piazza Venezia were demolished to make way for the Altare della Patria, also known as the Monumento Nazionale a Vittorio Emanuele II, built in honour of King Victor Emmanuel. The main consequence of this work was the destruction of the medieval district where Michelangelo's house stood. The only record we have of this area's special charm comes from a number of engravings and old photographs.

** This façade of the house said to be Michelangelo's formerly in Via delle Tre Pile and demolished in 1930 was rebuilt to grace the public highway 21 April 1941.*

A STATUE FACING THE OTHER WAY AT THE REQUEST OF THE VATICAN

On the Janiculum Hill, at one of the sites with the best views of Rome, an equestrian statue of Garibaldi stands on a high marble plinth, dominating the city spread out at his feet. This bronze monument by the artist Enrico Gallori, erected in 1895, has however had its ups and downs. Under Mussolini's dictatorship it was replaced by fascist symbols, but was eventually reinstalled in 1943, although in a different position, giving rise to a string of political interpretations. When the monument was first erected, the 'Hero of the Two Worlds' did indeed face the Vatican in a rather provocative way. At the time, the relationship between the fledgling Italian state and the Holy See was extremely tense and the Church felt that the unification of Italy was detrimental to its interests. With the signing of the Lateran Treaty in 1929 and the establishment of normal relations between the two states, the Holy See asked that the statue should face the city: the request was granted. The Romans were greatly amused, joking that now it is the horse's turn to show its backside to the Vatican! A crown on the steps to the right of the plinth is a reminder that the Republican Garibaldi was the first Grand Master of Italian Freemasonry.

04.

Villa Farnesina
Via della Lungara, 230
Bus 280 – Lungotevere Farnesina/Trilussa

HERMETIC FRESCOES OF VILLA FARNESINA

The 'lucky star' of Agostino Chigi

Villa Farnesina was built between 1508 and 1511 by Baldassare Peruzzi for the Sienese banker Agostino Chigi (1466–1520), then the richest man in Rome. It was later sold to the Farnese family, who gave it their name (see page 158 for the villa's history).
Chigi was interested in the mythological and esoteric themes for which there was quite a craze at this period of the Italian Renaissance. He asked Peruzzi (1481–1536) to paint a fresco of his horoscope, following a mythological and astrological journey. The result is a unique work that can still be seen today.
Conscious of being born 'under a lucky star', Chigi wanted his good fortune to be represented in his home by the favourable conjunctions of the stars on the day of his birth. In a work probably dated 1 December 1466, on the vaulted ceiling of the room on the ground floor of the villa (now the Galatea Room), Peruzzi sketched out the complete cycle of constellations and the planets aligned in a specific astrological pattern, symbolised by classical mythological figures on a background of intense blue sky.
Thus to illustrate the moment of Chigi's birth, he painted the constellation of the Great Bear aligned with those of Pegasus and Leo. In the centre of the ceiling vault is the fluttering winged figure of Fame. Perseus seizes and beheads the Gorgon, and from his blood springs Pegasus, the mythical winged horse of the constellation of the same name. Nearby, a chariot pulled by magnificent bulls carries a young girl up to heaven: Callisto, a nymph beloved of Jupiter whom he transformed into the constellation of Ursa Major (Great Bear) to escape the wrath of his wife Hera, who in a fit of jealousy had changed her into a she-bear. In the next hexagon, Hercules battles the Nemean Lion, suggesting the constellation of Leo.
Europa (who took the form of a bull after being ab-

ducted by Zeus), shown together with the symbolic representation of the ram, indicates that at the time of Chigi's birth the planet Jupiter (Zeus) was in the sign of Aries.

The Sun in Sagittarius is represented by Apollo near a centaur ready to let fly his arrow. The transit of the planet Venus in the constellation of Capricorn is illustrated by the goddess at the centre of a shell surrounded by doves and accompanied by the unicorn.

The artist continues the mythological story through signs of the Zodiac linked to Chigi: Gemini is denoted by the fable of the love of Zeus – in the form of a swan – for Leda, Queen of Sparta. From their union were born the Dioscuri (Sons of Zeus), the twins (Gemini) Castor and Pollux.

Hercules, bitten by a scorpion while fighting the monstrous Hydra, represents Scorpio; while Ganymede is ravished by Jupiter disguised as an eagle that carries him off to Olympus to be the cupbearer of the gods, symbolising Aquarius.

The traditional sequence of the signs of the Zodiac ends with Pisces, where Eros and Psyche are transformed, according to myth, to escape the monstrous Typhon.

The depiction of a favourable event as a ceiling fresco was more than just decoration, it had a real esoteric objective. According to the Egyptian tradition of hermeticism, rediscovered during the Renaissance (see the following double page), the positive energy represented by the fresco was supposed to pour into the room and into the entire house in which it was painted, as well as on the occupants.

HERMES TRISMEGISTUS AND HERMETISM

Hermes Trismegistus, which in Latin means 'thrice-great Hermes', is the name given by the neo-Platonists, alchemists, and Hermeticists to the Egyptian god *Thoth*, *Hermes* to the Greeks.

In the Old Testament, he is also identified with the patriarch Enoch. In their respective cultures, all three were considered to be the creators of phonetic writing, theurgical magic, and messianic prophetism. *Thoth* was connected to the lunar cycles whose phases expressed the harmony of the universe.

Egyptian writings refer to him as 'twice great' because he was the god of the Word and of Wisdom. In the syncretic atmosphere of the Roman Empire, the epithet of the Egyptian god *Thoth* was given to the Greek god *Hermes*, but this time was 'thrice great' (trismegistus) for the Word, Wisdom and his duty as Messenger of all the gods of the Elysium or of Olympus. The Romans associated him with Mercury, the planet that mediates between the Earth and the Sun, which is a function that Kabbalistic Jews called *Metatron*, the 'perpendicular measure between the Earth and the Sun'. In Hellenic Egypt, Hermes was the 'scribe and messenger of the gods' and was believed to be the author of a collection of sacred texts, called hermetic, that contained teachings about art, science, religion and philosophy – the *Corpus Hermeticum* – the objective of which was the deification of humanity through knowledge of God. These texts, which were probably written by a group belonging to the *Hermetic School* of ancient Egypt, thus express the knowledge accumulated over time by attributing it to the god of Wisdom, who is in all points similar to the Hindu god Ganesh. The *Corpus Hermeticum*, which probably dates from the 1st to the 3rd centuries CE, represented the source of inspiration of hermetic and neo-Platonic thought during the Renaissance. Even though Swiss scholar Casaubon had apparently proved the contrary in the 17th century, people continued to believe that the text dated back to Egyptian antiquity before Moses and that it announced the coming of Christianity. According to Clement of Alexandria, it contained 42 books divided into six volumes. The first treated the education of priests; the second, the rites of the temple; the third, geology, geography, botany and agriculture; the fourth, astronomy and astrology, mathematics and architecture; the fifth contained hymns to the glory of the gods and a guide of political action for kings; the sixth was a medical text. It is generally believed that Hermes Trismegistus invented a card game full of esoteric symbols, of which the first 22 were made of blades of gold and the 56 others of blades of silver – the tarot or 'Book of Thoth'. Hermes is also attributed with writing the *Book of the Dead* or *Book of the Exit* towards the Light, as well as the famous alchemy text *The Emerald Table*, works that had a strong influence on the alchemy and magic practised in medieval Europe. In medieval Europe, especially between the 5th and 14th centuries, hermetism was also a School of Hermeneutics that interpreted certain poems of antiquity and various enigmatic myths and works of art as allegorical treaties of alchemy or hermetic science. For this reason, the term hermetism still designates the esoteric nature of a text, work, word or action, in that they possess an occult meaning that requires a hermeneutic, or in other words a philosophical science, to correctly interpret the hidden meaning of the object of study. Hermetic principles were adopted and applied by the Roman Collegium Fabrorum, associations of the architects of civil, military and religious constructions. This knowledge was transmitted in the 12th century to the Christian builder-monks, the builders of the grand Roman and Gothic edifices of Europe, who executed their work according to the principles of sacred architecture, true to the model of sacred geometry. It is the direct legacy of volumes three and four of the *Corpus Hermeticum*, according to which cities and buildings were constructed in interrelation with specific planets and constellations, so that the design of the Heavens could be reproduced on Earth, thus favouring cosmic or sidereal energies. All of this was done with the purpose of achieving the hermetic principle that states: 'Everything above is like everything below'. During the European Renaissance (16th and 17th centuries), hermetism was replaced by humanism. Forms were rationalised and the transcendental ignored. It was the end of the traditional society and the beginning of a profane, Baroque and pre-modernist society, paving the way for the arrival of materialism and atheism that dominates the modern world. There were, however, some exceptions to this predominant rule in Europe. In Portugal, in the 16th century, the Master Builders, the heirs of the builder-monks, founded the Manueline style according to the hermetic rules of sacred architecture.

The influence of the Free Builders continued into the 18th century and their greatest work was the restoration of Lisbon after the earthquake of 1755. That is why Pombal's Lisbon is designed and constructed according to the geometric and architectural measures of the Tradition handed down by Hermes Trismegistus (see *Secret Lisbon* by the same publisher).

05.

Villa Farnesina
Via della Lungara, 230
Bus 280 – Lungotevere Farnesina/Trilussa

THE FACE AT VILLA FARNESINA

Michelangelo's alleged gift to Raphael

The banker Agostino Chigi entrusted the decoration of his Roman residence on the far side of the Tiber to the most renowned artists of the time: Peruzzi (who was also the architect) as well as Sebastiano del Piombo, Il Sodoma and Raphael. The only exception was Michelangelo as he was fully occupied with papal projects.
In the loggia featuring Raphael's *Triumph of Galatea* fresco is a magnificent charcoal study of a head that has long been attributed to Michelangelo. There have been several rumours about the origin of this drawing. It was said that Michelangelo was extremely curious about how the work was going, but Raphael had banned anyone from entering the loggia he was painting. To deceive the guards, Michelangelo disguised himself as a peddler and managed to enter the room where Raphael had been working. Then, unable to resist the temptation, he grabbed a stick of charcoal and drew a superb and imposing face in an unpainted alcove. Another version of the story is that Michelangelo wanted to see his pupil Daniele da Volterra, who was working on the Farnesina site. Not finding him, he climbed on the scaffolding to draw the head in question and left it to mark his visit. It's now thought that Baldassare Peruzzi, architect of the villa, must have made the drawing. This tale gives a sense of the intense rivalry in 16th-century Rome between all these outstanding artists.

The villa of Agostino Chigi 'the magnificent' was of proverbial beauty, but this did not last long. The building was occupied and damaged during the sack of Rome, then sold in 1581 by Chigi's bankrupt heirs to the Farnese family, who named it after themselves. But the gardens were later abandoned and the loggia overlooking the river was in ruins. The new owners eventually lost interest, as did the Bourbons of Naples who inherited the villa. The newly appointed Spanish ambassador bought it in 1870 and renovated a few rooms, but the hardest blow was dealt by the new Italian state: forty per cent of the land between the villa and the Tiber was requisitioned for river development projects. When the state finally acquired the villa in 1927, this architectural gem was in an appalling state of neglect and seemed unlikely to survive. Now spectacularly renovated, it is one of Rome's last surviving examples of a private Renaissance palace.

06.

Villa Farnesina
Via della Lungara, 230
Bus 280 – Lungotevere Farnesina/Trilussa

THE GRAFFITI OF CHARLES V'S SOLDIERS

A souvenir of the sacking of Rome in 1527

The lansquenets of Charles V, who sacked Rome in 1527, left their mark through numerous graffiti, notably at the Villa Farnesina and in the Raphael Rooms at the Vatican.

At the Farnesina, in the 'Hall of Perspectives' painted by Baldassare Peruzzi (1481–1536) and his pupils, graffiti appears within the painted cityscape on the north wall, between the painted columns. There, a mercenary etched the word Babilonia onto a Roman campanile using the point of his dagger. Rome, with its ostentatious material wealth funded by indulgences, was denounced by Lutherans as the new Babylon, destined for apocalyptic destruction.

Other graffiti can be seen on the fresco of the eastern wall. In the sky above the campanile of Santa Maria in Trastevere, an inscription scrawled in pencil reads: 'Why should I, who write this, not laugh? The lansquenets made the Pope run'. Dated 1528, this ironic farewell encapsulates the mercenaries' disdain for the city they had ravaged.

The lansquenets entered Rome on 6 May 1527, during the tumultuous years of the Italian Wars and amid mounting opposition to the power of the Roman Church. Martin Luther had published his Ninety-Five Theses in 1517, condemning the Church's sale of indulgences, and his excommunication in 1521 only heightened tensions.

The army of Charles V's mercenaries was commanded by the Constable of Bourbon, who was killed on the first day of the sack. Leaderless, the undisciplined and unpaid troops gave free rein to their instincts, with their survival dependent on looting. They laid siege to Pope Clement VII, who had taken refuge in Castel Sant'Angelo, defended by the cannons of Florentine artist and soldier Benvenuto Cellini (1500–1571). Over the following months, an army of approximately 23,000 soldiers – mostly Germans and Spaniards, but also some Italian bands – plunged the city into chaos, especially targeting papal buildings. This included the Raphael Rooms in the Vatican, where frescoes suffered considerable damage (see below).

GRAFFITI BY CHARLES V'S LANSQUENETS IN THE VATICAN

In the Vatican, graffiti is visible in the Stanza della Segnatura, where inscriptions such as *V. K. Imp.* (Charles V Emperor) and Luther appear on *The Disputation of the Holy Sacrament*. These inscriptions assert the lansquenets' identification with an antipapal crusade. Similarly, in the Stanza di Eliodoro, visitors can find *V. K. Imp.* alongside *Got hab dy sela Borbons* ('May God have Bourbon's soul'), a reference to the Constable of Bourbon.

07.

Villa Farnesina
Via della Lungara, 230
Bus 280 – Lungotevere Farnesina/Trilussa

THE GRAFFITI OF JACQUES-LOUIS DAVID

Even famous painters left graffiti

Within the Villa Farnesina, a surprising piece of graffiti is hidden in the fresco by Sodoma (1477–1549) depicting *The Marriage of Alexander and Roxana*. The Neoclassical painter Jacques-Louis David (1748–1825) discreetly signed his name in the folds of a servant's drapery.

A leading figure of Neoclassicism, David broke away from the playful and indulgent style of Rococo to, in his own words, 'regenerate the arts by creating a form of painting the Greek and Roman classics would unhesitatingly claim as their own'. During his time at the French Academy in Rome from 1775 to 1780, he studied ancient works with dedication. He returned to Rome in 1784, the same year he painted *The Oath of the Horatii* that would make him famous. It was during this second visit that he added his signature to Sodoma's fresco: 'louis David 1784'. The broad strokes of the 'd' are characteristic of the painter's signature.

This act, of course, compromises the integrity of the fresco. Could it be considered vandalism? Art historian Charlotte Guichard, in her work *Graffitis. Inscrire son nom à Rome. XVIe-XIXe siècle* (2014), cautions against such a reductive interpretation. She argues that a painter's act of inscribing their name on another's work is not mere defacement but carries deeper meaning. David's gesture pays homage to Sodoma's majestic style, itself drawing inspiration from antiquity. By writing his name into the fabric of the fresco, David positions himself within a lineage of artists, and claims a shared connection with Renaissance painters who revitalised the classical past. The act signifies both admiration for the original work and an assertion of mastery over its legacy.

David may have felt justified in his subtle signature, considering that the Villa had already been marked by graffiti since the Sack of Rome in 1527 (see previous double page). Furthermore, he placed his name just beneath that of Carlo Maratta (1625–1713), who signed 'Carlo Maratti' in the style of the registers of the Accademia di San Luca, of which he was a director. It was Maratta who restored the Farnesina frescoes in 1693, and then Raphael's Rooms and Lodges in the Vatican, which had been badly damaged during the Sack of Rome. By signing the fresco, David positions himself not merely as a visitor but as a Neoclassical restorer of painting, asserting his role in the continuation of its tradition.

TRASTEVERE

GIANICOLO
Santa Maria della Scala
Fontana dell' Acqua Paola
San Pietro in Montorio
Ospedale Nuovo Regina Margherita
TRASTEVERE
PIAZZA TRILUSSA
PIAZZA DE' RENZI
PIAZZA SAN EDIGIO
PIAZZA SANTA MARIA IN TRASTEVERE
PIAZZA SAN CALLISTO
PIAZZA G. TAVANI ARQUATI
PIAZZA SAN COSIMATO
PIAZZA MASTAI
PIAZZA SAN FRANCESCO D'ASSISI
PIAZZA BERNARDINO DA FELTRE
Lungotevere Raffaello Sanzio
Via Benedetta
Via della Scala
Via del Mattonato
Via dei Panieri
Via della Paglia
Via della Renella
Via della Lungaretta
Via G. Venezian
Via Luciano Manara
Via Natale del Grande
Via San Francesco a Ripa
Via di Porta Portese
Viale delle Mure Portuensi
Via C. Tavolacci
Via Goffredo Mameli
Via Dandolo
Via Garibaldi
Via Porta San Pancrazio
Passeggiata del Gianicolo
Via A. Masina
Via Giacomo Medici
Viale Trenta Aprile
Via Fabrizi
Via Nicola Fabrizi
Via Calandrelli
Via Filippo Casini
Viale Glorioso
Viale di Trastevere
Via San Gallicano
V. dei Fienaroli
Vicolo de' Cinque
Via del Politeama
Via del Moro
Villa Sciarra

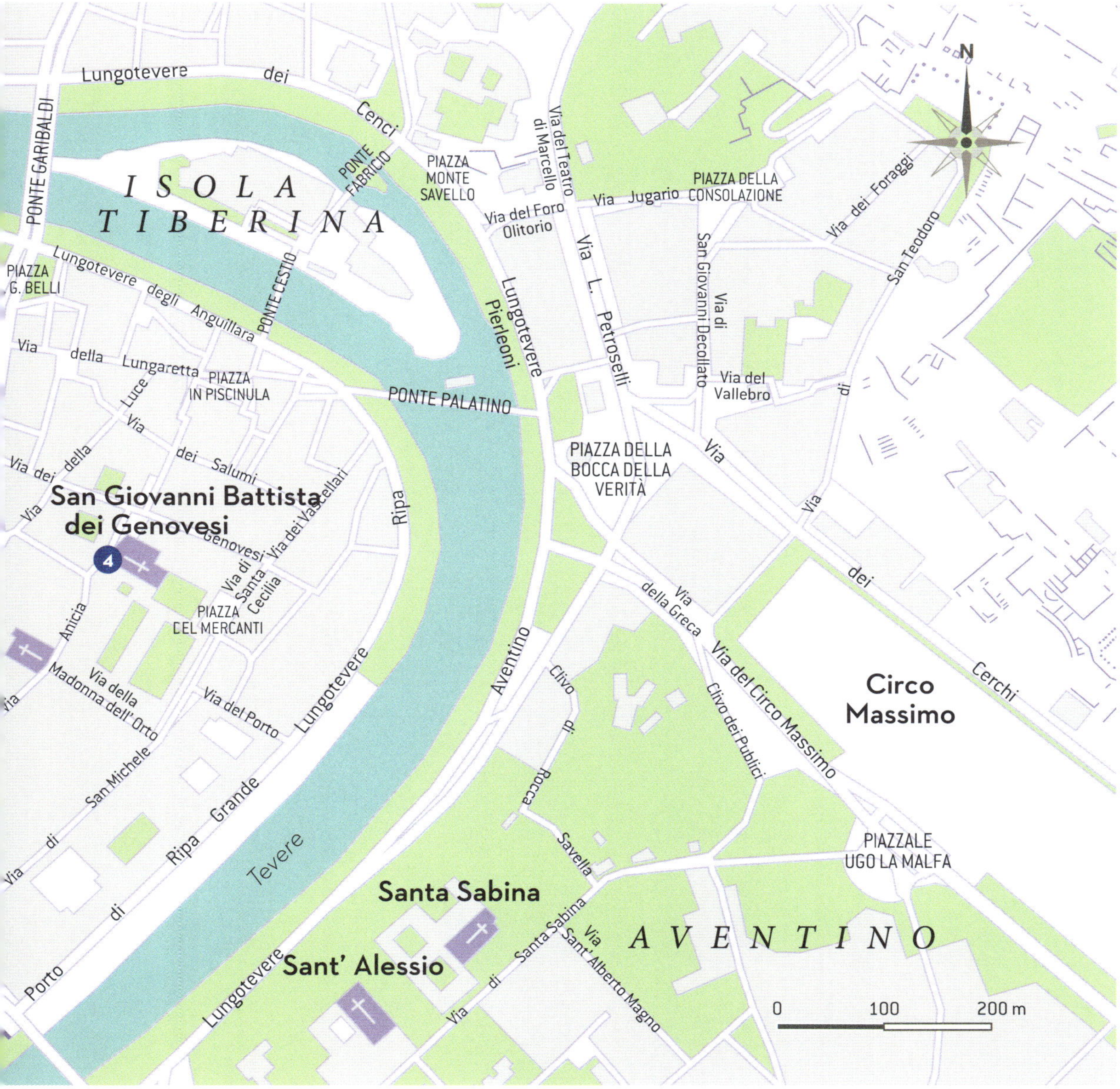

05. THE OLD PHARMACY OF SANTA MARIA DELLA SCALA *p. 174*

01.

San Francesco d'Assisi a Ripa Grande
Piazza San Francesco d'Assisi
Tram 3 – Induno; Bus H – Mastai

THE MECHANISM OF THE RELIQUARY OF SAINT FRANCIS' CELL

Relics hidden in a precious artefact

Saint Francis of Assisi and his disciples were lodged in a cell annexed to this church, which belonged to Benedictine monks before Pope Gregory IX asked them, in 1229, to hand it and the adjacent hospice over to the Order of Friars Minor (the Franciscans), who renamed it San Francesco d'Assisi a Ripa Grande.

It is not widely known that this cell, later converted into a chapel, holds a curious Baroque masterpiece: an amazing altar was carved from the roots of a walnut tree between 1698 and 1708 by the Franciscan brother Bernardino da Jesi, and later embellished with traditional paintings.

In the middle of the wood panelling is a magnificent 13th-century altarpiece featuring a portrait of Saint Francis attributed to the school of Margheritone d'Arezzo. The altarpiece is flanked by two 14th-century paintings depicting Saint Anthony of Padua and Saint Louis of Toulouse, while the side panels feature the Virgin and the Angel of the Annunciation, late 17th-century works by an artist of the school of Carlo Maratta. It was Cardinal Ranuccio Pallavicini who commissioned this rare artefact for the church, to which he also bequeathed his impressive collection of relics. The altarpiece in fact incorporates an ingenious mechanism: the relics are kept inside the altar, in precious silver coffers. When the mechanism is activated, all the visible parts pivot to reveal the treasures inside, thus transforming the altar into a sumptuous reliquary.

Next to the altar, in a niche closed by a grille, a stone on which Saint Francis is said to have laid his head has also been preserved.

02.

Piazza di San Cosimato
Tram 8 – Trastevere

THE CLOISTERS OF THE NUOVO REGINA MARGHERITA HOSPITAL

Hidden cloisters

The former monastery of Santi Cosma e Damiano in Mica Aurea, so named because it was built on the golden-coloured sand of the slopes of Janiculum Hill, later became known as San Cosimato. Today, it is part of the Nuovo Regina Margherita hospital complex, opened in 1970.

Apart from hospital staff, patients and their families, and passers-by, few people know that the hospital grounds contain two spectacular cloisters. The first is medieval, dating back to the beginning of the 12th century, and the other Renaissance, built during restoration work commissioned by Pope Sixtus IV.

The first cloister, which was one of the biggest in medieval Rome, is the most impressive. With arcades on all four sides, small twin columns supporting the narrow brick arches, the cloister is filled with fragments of ancient inscriptions. Columns and sarcophagi are scattered over the lawn and among the trees in the garden.

A few steps lead to the second cloister, square-shaped and smaller than the first. It is embellished with arcades of octagonal pilasters in travertine topped by lovely capitals carved with plant motifs. The interior garden features a water tank dating back to the mid-19th century.

San Cosimato, with its complex architectural history divided between two medieval periods and the Renaissance, was for centuries one of the richest monasteries in Rome.

The monastery, founded in the first half of the 10th century by Benedictine monks, was not completed until the 13th century. The Franciscan Order of Poor Clare nuns took over the convent in 1234 and had it enlarged. This was followed by work carried out under Pope Sixtus IV for the 1475 Jubilee, during which a new church, a belfry and the second cloister were constructed.

After the unification of Italy and the introduction of legislation suppressing religious corporations, the Italian state ceded San Cosimato convent to the City of Rome. It was granted to a charitable organisation and then converted into a hospice.

03.

Institute of Santa Maria and San Gallicano
Via San Gallicano, 25
Bus H – arrêt Mastai

ANATOMY THEATRE OF SAN GALLICANO HOSPITAL

A room for dissecting corpses

Within the constantly busy precincts of the Santa Maria e San Gallicano hospital can be found its former anatomy theatre. Here, in this room decorated with stucco bas-reliefs, dissections of human bodies used to be carried out. On the floor, below the light flooding from the pierced vault, a large marble slab marks the location of the table on which the corpses lay. The room is now the headquarters of the institute's scientific management.

Pope Leo XII had this anatomy theatre built in 1826 to celebrate the centenary of the Institute of Santa Maria and San Gallicano. The architect Giacomo Palazzi was commissioned to design this oval room at the centre of which opens onto a round vault surrounded by allegories of medicine. Around the sides, stucco medallions depict eighteen illustrious Roman doctors, from Celsus, known as the Latin Hippocrates (1st century CE) to the great anatomist Gabriele Fallopio (1523–1562) who described certain essential aspects of the reproductive and auditory systems, and Lancisi (1654-1720) who established the correlation between mosquitoes and malaria.

The main beauty of this room lies in the stucco bas-reliefs sculpted by Ignazio del Sarti, representing the legend of Asclepius as recounted in Ovid's *Metamorphoses* (see opposite).

WAS ASCLEPIUS, GOD OF MEDICINE, BEHIND THE CREATION OF TIBER ISLAND?

According to Ovid's account in *Metamorphoses*, when a great plague decimated the population of Rome, the Romans went to consult the oracle at Delphi. The prophetess replied that they needed the help of her son, the god of medicine, rather than Apollo. So the Roman Senate sent a delegation to fetch Asclepius by ship from Epidaurus. He told them that he would appear as a serpent and that they would need to recognise him in this form. The Romans prayed to the god and a great serpent appeared, which they allowed on board. The serpent dispelled the perils of the voyage and the ship sailed safely back up the Tiber. On arriving at Rome, the serpent wrapped itself around the trunk of a tree. At this very spot the river divided into two channels, creating an island. The serpent then slithered down from the tree and healed Rome's citizens.

There are also well-preserved anatomy theatres in Berlin, in London, Barcelona, Pistoia (Tuscany), Padua and Bologna. See *Secret Berlin*, *Secret London*, *Secret Tuscany* and *Secret Barcelona* from the same publisher.

04.

Via Anicia, 12
Tram 8 – Trastevere/Mastci

THE CLOISTER OF SAN GIOVANNI BATTISTA DEI GENOVESI

A little-known 15th-century marvel

Among the maze of buildings in the Trastevere district is the headquarters of the brotherhood of Saint John the Baptist, where one of the most beautiful cloisters in Rome is hidden from the street. Access is via the church through a little door in the left-hand wall.

You will find yourself in a haven of peace and silence, immediately entranced by the beauty of the ground-floor archways buttressed onto octagonal columns and the architraves of the upper storey, as well as the contrast between their shade and the luxuriant green plants bathed in sunshine. In the centre of the garden stands a 14th-century travertine well, set off by two antique columns in Ionic style.

Fragments of antique marble are scattered here and there beneath the arcades. The church and most of the buildings were given so many facelifts between the 15th and 19th centuries that they have lost their original appearance, with the exception of the old hospice and the cloister, built in 1481 and attributed to Baccio Pontelli, designer of the Sistine Chapel.

An inscription on a funerary stele explains that inside the cloister there used to be a compound, demolished at the end of the 18th century, while another inscription on a column, in Latin this time, says that in this cloister the very first palm tree to be imported to Rome was planted by a friar from Savona in the late 16th century.

The cycle of frescoes attributed to Guido Signorini and Gerolamo Margotti dates from the beginning of the 17th century, however. They were discovered in the 1970s under a thick coat of lime-washed plaster during the restoration of the site. The brotherhood was founded in 1533, although the church dedicated to Saint John the Baptist (patron saint of the city of Genoa) and its hospice (founded by Pope Sixtus IV and paid for by the Genoese ambassador to help sailors) already existed.

WHY IS JOHN THE BAPTIST THE PATRON SAINT OF GENOA?

Around the year 1100, on the way back to Genoa from the Crusades, Genoese sailors stopped off along the coast of Lycia (now south-western Turkey) and found the ashes of Saint John the Baptist in a convent, not far from the town of Myra (modern Demre). Following this episode, the town adopted the saint as its patron.

05.

Piazza Santa Maria della Scala
Tram 8 – Trastevere/Mastai; Bus 23, 280 – Lungotevere Farnesina/Trilussa

THE OLD PHARMACY OF SANTA MARIA DELLA SCALA

A 16th-century pharmacy

The Farmacia di Santa Maria della Scala, which was opened by Carmelites who arrived in Rome in the late 16th century, became famous among convent pharmacies thanks to the various specialities invented there to fight the plague and other serious diseases.
The pharmacy managed to keep a free dispensary open to the public until the 1950s and stayed open until 1978.
The upper floor of this old pharmacy has been preserved, above a more modern working establishment, virtually intact, as it was in the 18th century, and offers visitors a unique experience.
One of the monks working in the pharmacy, Brother Basil, became so well-known for his herbal remedies and especially for his famous Acqua Antipestilenziale (Anti-Plague Water), which cured various types of ailments, that kings, cardinals and popes consulted him. In 1726 he began to teach chemistry, botany and pharmacy to his disciples.
The eulogistic inscriptions on two paintings featuring this well-loved monk, who died in 1804 after almost 60 years of professional activity, sum up his life. His famous essays have been carefully preserved as precious artefacts.
Ghezzi's 18th-century painting, which is kept in the vestry, perfectly conveys the idea of the beauty and importance of the pharmacy at the time. It features Brother Basil teaching his disciples, surrounded by stills and mortars, shelves overflowing with heavy tomes, and cupboards with jars filled with salts and herbs.

HVARTETICH
POL.MONT
FLOR.HIPER

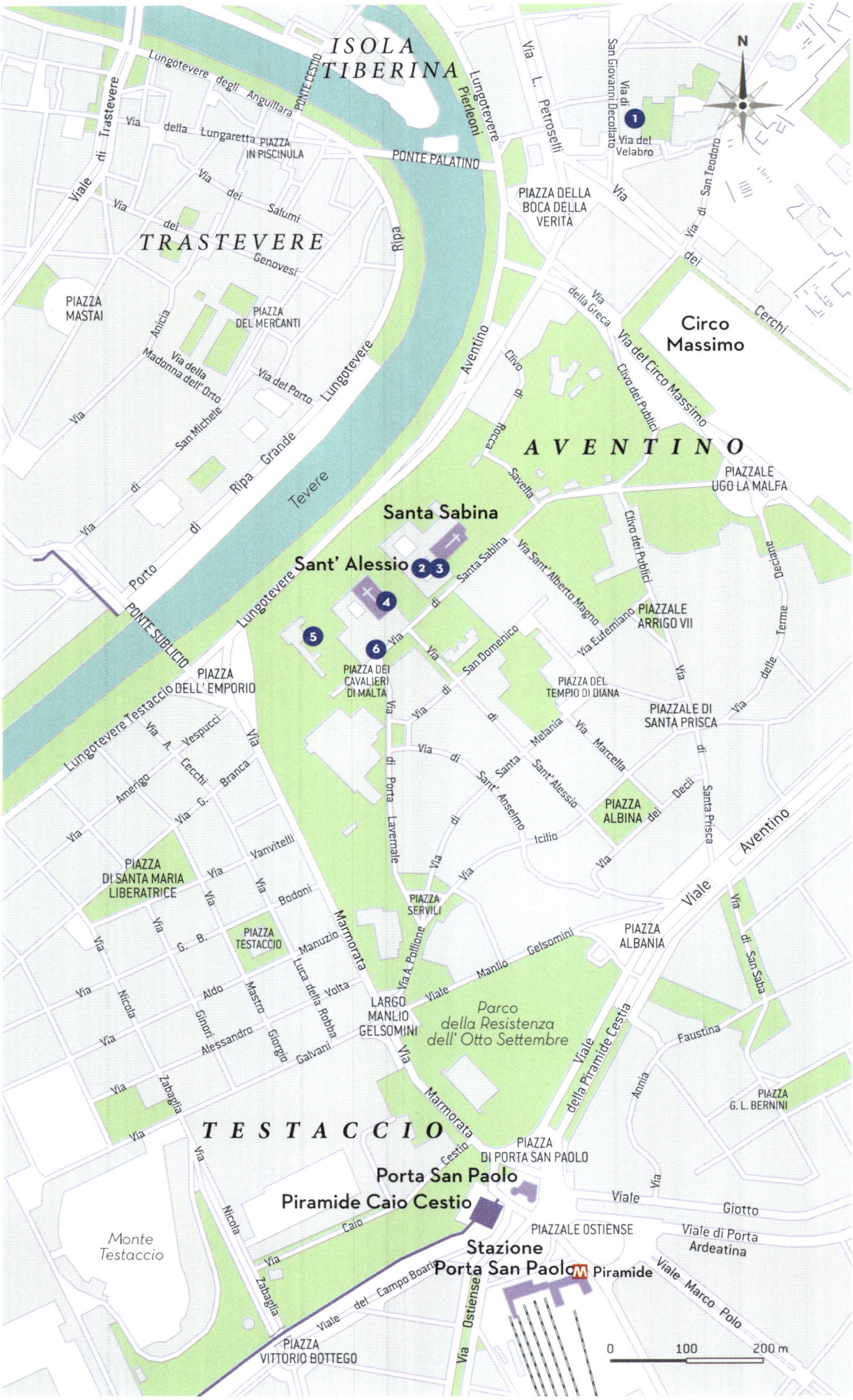
N
ISOLA TIBERINA
TRASTEVERE
AVENTINO
TESTACCIO
Circo Massimo
Santa Sabina
Sant' Alessio
Porta San Paolo
Piramide Caio Cestio
Stazione Porta San Paolo
Piramide
Monte Testaccio
Parco della Resistenza dell' Otto Settembre
Tevere
PONTE CESTIO
PONTE PALATINO
PONTE SUBLICIO
PIAZZA IN PISCINULA
PIAZZA MASTAI
PIAZZA DEL MERCANTI
PIAZZA DELLA BOCA DELLA VERITÀ
PIAZZALE UGO LA MALFA
PIAZZALE ARRIGO VII
PIAZZA DELL' EMPORIO
PIAZZA DEI CAVALIERI DI MALTA
PIAZZA DEL TEMPIO DI DIANA
PIAZZALE DI SANTA PRISCA
PIAZZA ALBINA
PIAZZA DI SANTA MARIA LIBERATRICE
PIAZZA TESTACCIO
PIAZZA SERVILI
PIAZZA ALBANIA
LARGO MANLIO GELSOMINI
PIAZZA G. L. BERNINI
PIAZZA DI PORTA SAN PAOLO
PIAZZALE OSTIENSE
PIAZZA VITTORIO BOTTEGO
Lungotevere degli Anguillara
Lungotevere Pierleoni
Lungotevere Testaccio
Viale di Trastevere
Via della Lungaretta
Via dei Salumi
Via dei Genovesi
Via Anicia
Via della Madonna dell' Orto
Via del Porto
Via di San Michele
Via di Ripa Grande
Porto di Ripa Grande
Via L. Petroselli
Via di San Giovanni Decollato
Via del Velabro
Via di San Teodoro
Via dei Cerchi
Via della Greca
Via del Circo Massimo
Clivo dei Publici
Clivo di Rocca Savella
Lungotevere Aventino
Via di Santa Sabina
Via Sant' Alberto Magno
Via Eufemiano
Via di San Domenico
Via di Porta Lavernale
Via di Santa Melania
Via Marcella
Via di Sant' Anselmo
Via Sant' Alessio
Via dei Decii
Via di Santa Prisca
Via Icilio
Viale Aventino
Via delle Terme Deciane
Via A. Vespucci
Via Cecchi
Via G. Branca
Via Amerigo
Via Vanvitelli
Via Bodoni
Via G. B.
Via Manuzio
Via Luca della Robbia
Via Marmorata
Via Mastro Giorgio
Via Volta
Via Galvani
Via Nicola
Via Aldo
Via Ginori
Via Alessandro
Via Zabaglia
Via A. Pollione
Viale Manlio Gelsomini
Viale della Piramide Cestia
Via di San Saba
Via Annia
Via Faustina
Via Cestio
Via Caio
Viale del Campo Boario
Via Ostiense
Viale Giotto
Viale di Porta Ardeatina
Viale Marco Polo
0
100
200 m
1
2
3
4
5
6

AVENTINO – TESTACCIO

01.

Arco degli Argentarii
Via del Velabro
Metro B – Circo Massimo; Bus 51, 81, 85, 87 – Cerchi/Bocca della verità

THE FIGURES MISSING FROM THE ARCH OF THE MONEYCHANGERS

Fratricide between the sons of Septimius Severus

Just beside the ancient church of San Giorgio al Velabro stands an arch known as the Arco degli Argentarii (Arch of the Moneychangers), for it was the moneychangers of Rome who together with the meat merchants dedicated this monumental gateway to the emperor Septimius Severus.

The arch was not simply ornamental but probably served as one of the main points of access to the Forum Boarium, the ancient cattle market. Rich decoration with plant motifs covers almost the entire surface of the pillars and architrave. You can still read the original inscription, with the dedication dating from 204 CE to Septimius Severus, his wife Julia Domna and his son Bassianus, better known as Caracalla. The nickname came from a floor-length cloak he had made fashionable. The inner faces of the pillars show Caracalla carrying out a religious sacrifice, on the left, and the imperial family, on the right.

If you look more closely you will see among these images empty spaces where other figures have been deliberately obliterated.

After the death of Septimius Severus and according to his wishes, his two sons Caracalla and Geta governed together for almost a year, until Geta was assassinated by his brother, in their mother's arms, according to Aelius Spartianus's account in his *History of Augustus*. Caracalla accused Geta of attempting to poison him and the senate was obliged to believe this story, declaring Geta henceforth a public enemy and sentencing him to *damnatio memoriae*, a sanction that meant his image would be destroyed and his name erased from all inscriptions.

This enabled Caracalla to erase the name and portrait of his murdered brother, who had certainly been shown alongside his parents, as well as those of his wife Plautilla and his father-in-law, the praetorian prefect Plautianus (commander of the imperial guard).

THE HOLES IN THE ARCH OF THE MONEYCHANGERS

Another notable feature of the back of the arch is a number of holes, drilled in the Middle Ages. They were made by fortune-seekers who believed the story that a great treasure was hidden inside.

02.

Basilica di Santa Sabina,
Piazza Pietro D'Illiria, 1
Metro B – Circo Massimo

THE ORANGE TREE OF SANTA SABINA CLOISTER

The legend of Saint Dominic's orange tree

Santa Sabina Basilica, on the Aventine Hill, dates from the 5th century. It is one of the oldest churches in Rome, although it has frequently undergone major restorations since it was built. In the atrium, by a small oval window opening onto the courtyard of the neighbouring convent, an orange tree can be glimpsed growing in the very spot where, according to Dominican traditions, Saint Dominic planted it around 1220.
A number of anecdotes concerning this orange tree, more or less apocryphal, have endured down the ages. One notable claim is that Saint Dominic brought it back from Spain and planted it at the north-west corner of the former four-arched portico (no longer standing) where he liked to sleep. Until then, oranges had never been known to grow in Italy.
For centuries, this tree was described as miraculous, a new plant perennially springing from the desiccated trunk. Saint Francis de Sales (1567–1622) mentioned it in a letter to Saint Jane Frances de Chantal, in which he demonstrated how the tree had become a focus of the cult of Saint Dominic. Its oranges are said to have been used to make garlands and mementoes for popes and cardinals. And the story goes that the preserved oranges that Catherine of Siena offered to Urban VI in 1379 came from this miraculous tree.
In 1936, the ground was levelled where the tree grew. During the work, a coin dating from the 14th century was found among its roots.

NAPOLEON ON A 5TH-CENTURY DOOR!

Carved in the 5th century CE, the famous wooden panels covering the church door depict scenes from the Old and New Testaments. Curiously enough, a portrait of Napoleon can be seen there, shown as the pharaoh pursuing the Jews at the crossing of the Red Sea.
In fact, in the first half of the 19th century, a sculptor restoring the door had taken it upon himself to depict Napoleon as a persecutor of God's chosen people.
The reality was somewhat different, however, concerning Napoleon and the Jews: he was the first European monarch to liberate them from their ghettos, such as the one in Venice, and to grant them certain rights.

03.

Basilica di Santa Sabina,
Piazza Pietro D'Illiria, 1
Metro B – Circo Massimo

THE DEVIL'S STONE

A magical black stone?

If you have never been close to an object cast by the Devil, just go into the basilica of Santa Sabina by the main entrance and walk round to the left: at the corner, on top of a beautiful twisted column, you will see a black stone thought to have magical powers. It is in fact a well-preserved basalt counterweight dating from Roman times.

In 1586, Pope Sixtus V (1585–1590) commissioned the architect Domenico Fontana to restore the church. During the renovations – to which there were many objections – the architect had a marble slab commemorating the removal of the mortal remains of the martyrs Alexander, Evence and Theodule lifted from the floor. Unfortunately the slab fell and shattered into a thousand pieces, which were later collected and reassembled at the centre of what is now the Schola Cantorum. However, popular legend turned the story on its head to say that the marble slab was destroyed by a terrible black stone – lapis diaboli – launched by the Devil himself to strike St Dominic while he was deep in prayer over the martyrs' tomb.

The basilica of Santa Sabina was founded under the papacy of Celestine I (422–432) by Bishop Peter of Illyria. Excavations under the building have unearthed ancient structures from various periods. Materials plundered from nearby Roman ruins were used in the construction of the church, such as the twenty-four columns separating the three naves which come from the temple of Juno. In the 9th century, Pope Eugenius II (824–827) had the Schola Cantorum built and commissioned a silver ciborium to be placed there, which was unfortunately stolen by lansquenets mercenaries during the 1527 sack of Rome.

In 1219, Pope Honorius III donated Santa Sabina to the Spanish founder of the Dominican order, Domingo de Guzmán (Saint Dominic).

THE OLDEST KNOWN CRUCIFIXION SCENE

The front doors of the church, made of cypress wood, date back to its founding in the 5th century. They feature scenes from the Old and New Testaments, including the oldest known representation of the Crucifixion of Christ.

For centuries the basilica has been the first station of Lent where, on Ash Wednesday (the first day of penance and fasting), the pontiffs give their homily 44 days before Easter.

04.

Church of Santi Boniface e Alessio
Piazza Sant'Alessio, 23
Metro B – Circo Massimo

THE HIDING PLACE OF SAINT ALEXIUS

The saint who lived under the stairs

In a chapel of the church of Saints Boniface and Alexius, on the Aventine Hill, part of the wooden staircase under which Saint Alexius lived for 17 years has been preserved.

Before the 10th century, there is no record of Saint Alexius in the West, but from then on his celebrity became such that he inspired frescoes (a fine example of which is conserved in the Lower Basilica of San Clemente), poems and pieces of music which have fascinating histories.

Alexius was miraculously born to noble but barren parents in Rome. Although raised in the lap of luxury, he fled to Odessa in the East, where he lived on charity for several years as an ascetic. When his reputation for sanctity grew to be a burden, Alexius decided to leave and sail to Tarsus, but the direction of the wind, or perhaps destiny, took him instead to Ostia. He headed for Rome and presented himself at his father's house. His father welcomed him without recognising him; thinking that he was a beggar, he offered shelter beneath the staircase. Alexius lived there for 17 years and wrote his life story on a roll of paper. Only when he died did his family discover his true identity, revealed in the scroll that he still clutched in his hand.

The church dates back to the 4th century, when Pope Honorius III ordered the reconstruction of a building dedicated to Saint Boniface already erected on the Aventine. In 1217, it was also dedicated to Saint Alexius.

The plan of the church, which owes its current appearance to restorations of the 16th, 17th and 19th centuries, is a replica of the Roman building with three naves, where you can still see the belltower and crypt (which has a fresco painted between the 13th and 14th centuries, the only example of its kind in Rome) whence came the fragment of staircase preserved in the chapel of Sant'Alessio.

Antonio Bergondi, apprentice sculptor to Bernini, executed a marble statue for this chapel, representing the saint as a pilgrim on his deathbed.

In the church there is also a well that, it is said, formerly stood within the house of Alexius' father, as well as the 3rd century icon of the Assumption of Mary, which legend has it the saint brought back from the East.

05.

Piazza dei Cavalieri di Malta
Metro B – Circo Massimo

GARDENS OF THE KNIGHTS OF MALTA PRIORY

The ancient garden of the Templars

The origins of the priory date back to the 10th century, when as Santa Maria Aventina it formed part of a Benedictine abbey dedicated to Saint Basil of Cappadocia. In the 12th century, the abbey passed into the hands of the Templars and, at the beginning of the 14th century, to the Knights of Rhodes – later known as the Knights of Malta.

Today, you can overcome the frustration born of peering through the priory keyhole (see below), as group visits can be booked to tour the priory and its grounds. Access is by a magnificent although relatively small garden, whose exoticism gives it a heady air of romance. In one corner of the garden, a well built by the Templars still survives, the only vestige of their passing. You can also visit the church of Santa Maria del Priorato, built in the 16th century. It is the only architectural work – apart from the piazza – carried out by Piranesi. The single-nave interior has been entirely covered in white stucco to his design, and the façade offers a typical example of Piranesian style.

THE ORDER OF MALTA'S KEYHOLE

The Piazza dei Cavalieri di Malta (Square of the Knights of Malta) is encircled by palm and cypress trees and flamboyant walls, rich in steles and obelisks, designed by Giovanni Battista Piranesi.

The monumental entrance to the priory, headquarters of the Knights of Malta, seems to conceal a mysterious and unapproachable world but even the outside has a surprise in store. By placing your eye to the keyhole of the main entrance, the dome of St Peter's Basilica can be seen, framed by an avenue of luxuriant greenery within the walled gardens.

The Grand Prior Giovan Battista Rezzonico commissioned Piranesi to design the site, property of the Sovereign Order of Malta.

THE ORDER OF MALTA: THE ONLY PRIVATE INSTITUTION IN THE WORLD WITH THE ATTRIBUTES OF A SOVEREIGN STATE EXTRATERRITORIALITY, EMBASSIES ...

The Sovereign Military and Hospitaller Order of St John of Jerusalem, of Rhodes, and of Malta, more commonly known down the ages as the Knights Hospitaller, Order of the Knights of Rhodes, and Order of Malta, is one of the most ancient Roman Catholic religious orders whose current mission is to defend the faith and assist the poor and needy.

Founded in Jerusalem around 1050 by merchants of the former republic of Amalfi to care for pilgrims in the Holy Land, this monastic community dedicated to John the Baptist was recognised as a religious order by Pope Paschal II in 1113.

The Hospitallers rapidly became militarised after the taking of Jerusalem during the First Crusade of 1099, second only to the Templars as a fighting force in the Holy Land. After the fall of Jerusalem and Saint-Jean-d'Acre in 1291, the Order retreated to Cyprus from 1291 to 1309. As the knights' rivalry with the King of Cyprus was creating difficulties, they conquered the island of Rhodes, then under Byzantine rule, and made it their new headquarters in 1310, ruling there until 1523. The island situation led them to acquire a fleet that became the scourge of Muslim shipping. Eventually vanquished by the Turks, the knights sailed to Civitavecchia and then Viterbo, in Italy, before travelling to Nice and in 1530 finally settling in Malta, given to them by the Holy Roman Emperor Charles V who had understood how useful they could be against any Ottoman advances. But Napoleon drove them out when he occupied the island in 1798, and they were finally welcomed in Rome by the pope in 1834.

Before the loss of Malta, most members of the order were monks who had taken the three vows of poverty, chastity and obedience. Even today some members are monks, but most of the knights and dames that now make up the Order are lay members (there are 11,000 of them). The military function has not been exercised since 1798.

Although, in the past, the knights of the Order had to come from chivalrous and noble Christian families, current members need only distinguish themselves by their faith, morality and the virtues sought within the Church and the Order itself. Although volunteers are always welcome, you can only become a member by invitation.

The Order maintains diplomatic relations with 100 countries through its embassies. It has a very special status, making it the only private institution that is treated almost like a country in itself. Activities are financed by donations from members and other private parties. Its headquarters are at two sites in Rome, which have been granted extraterritoriality. These are Palazzo di Malta at 68 Via dei Condotti, where the grand master resides and meets with government bodies, and Villa Malta on the Aventine Hill, which houses the Grand Priory of Rome, the Embassy of the Order to the Holy See and the Embassy of the Order to the Italian Republic.

THE MALTESE CROSS

Founded in 11th-century Jerusalem by merchants from Amalfi (near Naples), the Sovereign Order of the Knights Hospitaller of St John of Jerusalem (the future Knights of Malta) first took the symbol of Amalfi's port (without its blue background) to be theirs. Then, in 1130, Raymond de Puy converted the charitable brotherhood into a military Order and won the right to use a white cross from Pope Innocent II; the colour was chosen to avoid confusion with the Templars' red cross.
Shortly after the Turks drove them off the island of Rhodes in 1523, the Order settled on Malta.
At that point, the island's red flag, inherited from the period of Norman occupation, became the background to the white cross, thus creating the Maltese Cross.

THE MEANING OF THE EIGHT POINTS IN THE MALTESE CROSS

The eight points in the Maltese Cross signify various things:
- the eight sides of the Dome of the Rock at Jerusalem.
- the eight nationalities of the original knights of the Order of St John of Jerusalem (the future Order of Malta) or the eight principles they undertook to live by: spirituality, simplicity, humility, compassion, justice, pity, sincerity and patience.
- the eight virtues which a knight of the Order of Malta was expected to possess: loyalty, pity, frankness, courage, honour, contempt of death, solidarity with the sick and poor, respect for the Catholic Church.
- the Eight Beatitudes which Christ listed in his Sermon on the Mount (St Matthew's Gospel, Chapter 5):
Blessed are the poor in spirit: for theirs is the kingdom of heaven. (Verse 3)
Blessed are the meek: for they shall possess the land. (Verse 4)
Blessed are they who mourn: for they shall be comforted. (Verse 5)
Blessed are they that hunger and thirst after justice: for they shall have their fill. (Verse 6)
Blessed are the merciful: for they shall obtain mercy. (Verse 7)
Blessed are the clean of heart: for they shall see God. (Verse 8)
Blessed are the peacemakers: for they shall be called the children of God. (Verse 9)
Blessed are they that suffer persecution for justice' sake, for theirs is the kingdom of heaven. (Verse 10)

06.

Piazza dei Cavalieri di Malta, 2
Metro B – Circo Massimo

ISTITUTO NAZIONALE DI STUDI ROMANI

A heaven of peacebiscuit

The priory in Piazza dei Cavalieri di Malta, a Piranesi masterpiece, is well known as the Rome headquarters of the Knights of Malta. No. 2, the National Institute of Roman Studies, is also a small haven of peace that should not be missed. It is housed in one of Rome's major monastic centres from the High Middle Ages, the monastery of Saints Boniface and Alexius, thought to have been built around the 7th century on the ruins of an imposing Roman sanctuary. The present building dates mainly from the 17th and 18th centuries, with restructuring work by the architect Giovanni Battista Nolli. At the entrance is a large square courtyard with archaeological remains. The heart of the former monastery is the 16th-century cloister, built by reusing antique columns of marble and granite, topped with capitals, each one different from the others. An entire wing of the building overlooks the Tiber, and a loggia leads to a vast panoramic garden. From there, you can go in and admire the few remaining – though very interesting – decorations.
The ceiling of the Sala di Presidenza (Hall of the Presidency), the former library, has a fresco dating from 1754 entitled *Allegory of the Progress of the Sciences and the Arts*, covering the main themes dear to the Enlightenment. The rest of the main floor was occupied by Charles IV of Spain who, driven from his country by Napoleon's troops, took refuge in Rome and decided to settle here. The apartments are adorned with marble floors and Pompeian-style frescoes.

GIOVANNI BATTISTA NOLLI: ARCHITECT CARTOGRAPHER

History teems with stories of polymath scientists or artists. Giovanni Battista Nolli (1692–1756) is a prime example. He was trained as a surveyor but became interested in astronomy and mathematics. On joining the court of the Albani and Corsini families, he rubbed shoulders with scholars and scientists and decided to fill a gap by drawing up the first modern map of Rome. With the support of Pope Benedict XIV, the help of his son and the collaboration of Piranesi and Giuseppe Vasi, he obtained permission to enter all the city's private properties, including the monasteries, to survey their records. His new map, the *Nuova Topografia*, was published in 1744. He was also a practising architect (see opposite).

The National Institute of Roman Studies was founded in 1925 as a private initiative by Carlo Galazzi Paluzzi, a great lover of Roman history. Public interest soon grew, and since 1951 the institute has been seen as a cultural and scientific centre for the research and dissemination of anything that furthers the knowledge of Rome, from antiquity to the present day. To this end it organises congresses, conferences and visits, maintains a well-endowed library and publishes the journal *Studi romani* (Roman Studies). It also runs the *Certamen Capitolinum* Latin prose and poetry competition, whose programme, incidentally, is published in Latin.

LATRAN – COLOSSEUM – FORUM

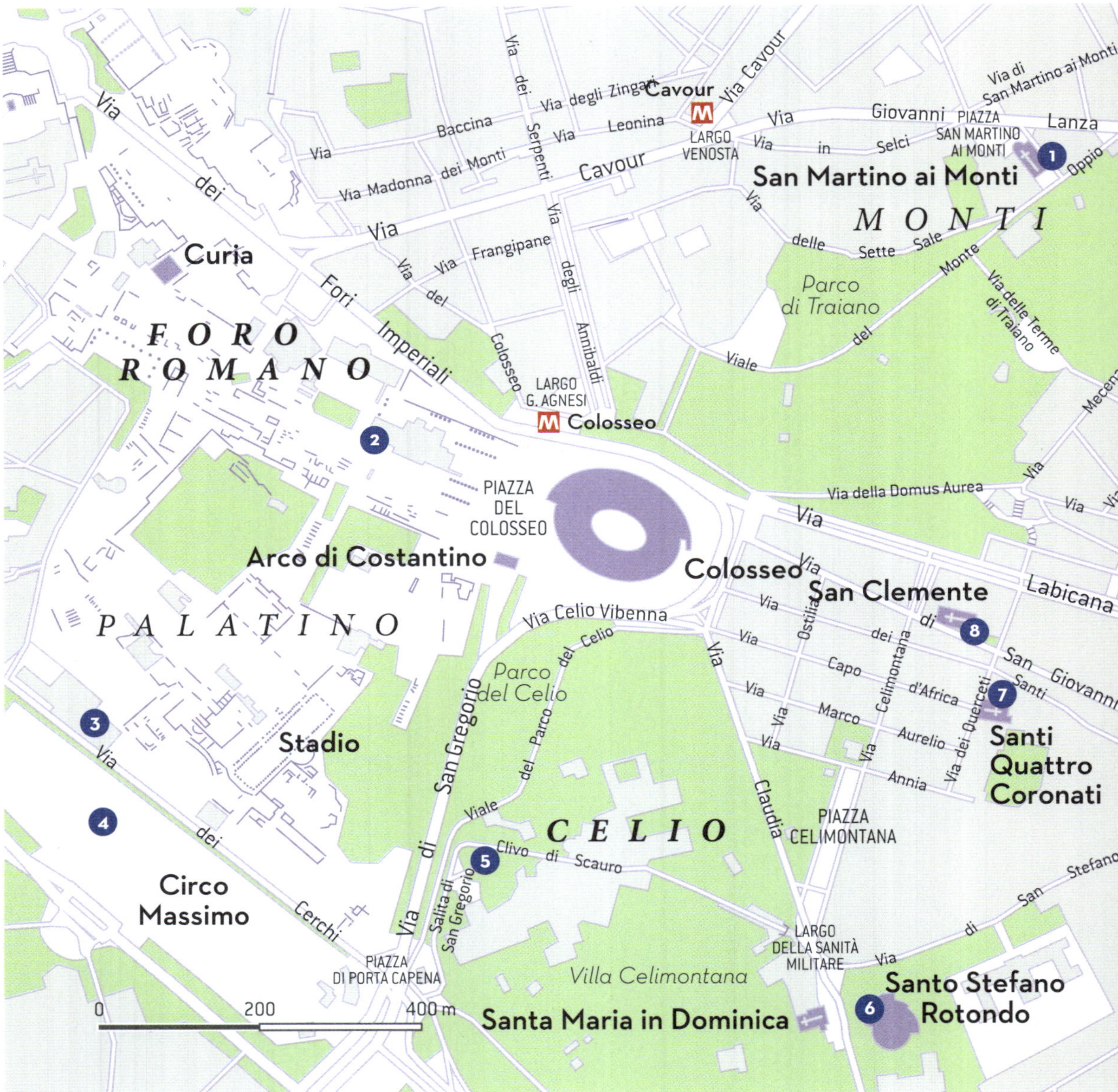

– CELIO

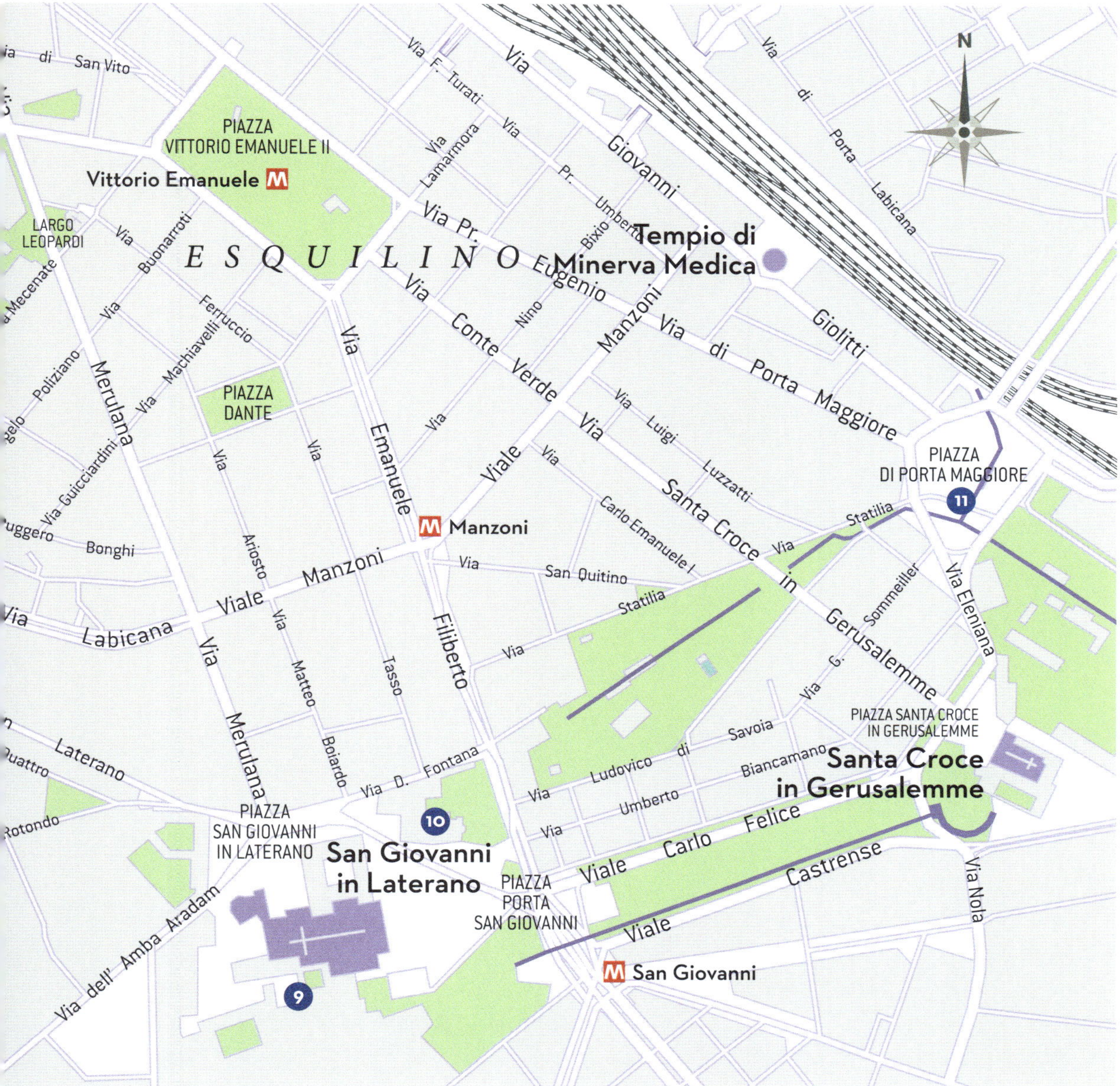

07. GAME IN THE CLOISTER OF SANTI QUATTRO CORONATI BASILICA *p. 208*

08. VERBAL ABUSE IN BASILICA SAN CLEMENTE *p. 210*

09. THE TRIPLE ENCLOSURES OF SAN GIOVANNI IN LATERANO CLOISTER *p. 214*

10. THE RELIC OF CHRIST'S FORESKIN *p. 216*

11. THE BAKER'S TOMB *p. 220*

01.

Via del Monte Oppio, 28
Metro B – Cavour

TITULUS EQUITII BELOW THE BASILICA OF SAN MARTINO AI MONTI

One of the most interesting constructions of early Christian Rome

On the slopes of Colle Oppio, the basilica of San Martino ai Monti (Saint Martin of the Mountains) has one of the most interesting constructions of early Christian Rome preserved in its crypt.

Since excavations were carried out in 1637, a series of chambers has been discovered whose original use is disputed because of the numerous transformations they have undergone over the centuries.

On the outside, along Via Equizia, the change in level between apse and façade is offset by a massive wall composed of blocks of volcanic tufa, perhaps quarried from the ramparts known as the Mura Serviane (Servian Wall).

Once inside the church, you cross the central nave to a staircase leading down into a Baroque crypt beneath the main altar. From there, through a door to the left, is another stairway that gives access to a large rectangular brick-built hall, 14 by 17 metres, divided into three naves by six pillars. The original cladding is still there, with lattice vaults reinforced by concrete joists. This construction, which dates back to the 3rd century CE, used to be part of the neighbouring Baths of Trajan. Afterwards it was probably used for commercial purposes such as a covered market or a warehouse. Some scholars, however, believe it may have been a rich man's house (*domus*). From the late 3rd century, it is thought that it was used as a meeting place by the early Christians.

It was Pope Sylvester I (314–335 CE) who founded the basilica on this property, donated by one Equitius, hence the name *Titulus Equitii*, converting it to the requirements of the Christian rite at communal meetings.

It soon became a site of major importance for the Christian Church: the Synods of 499 CE and 595 CE were both held here.

The church above was built in the 9th century, and the crypts were restored and embellished at the same time. Certain sections of painting that can still be seen on the vaulting are from this period: scenes of saints surrounded by the Virgin and Jesus, whose postures and strikingly coloured clothing are typical of Byzantine art. Fragments of mosaic are also visible on the black-and-white paving, which along with the ornamental motifs of some of the frescoes, seems to date from the early 3rd century, at the time when the site was still in commercial use.

A second flight of steps leads to other underground chambers, unfortunately completely buried.

02.

Church of Santa Francesca Romana
Piazza Santa Francesca Romana
Metro B – Colosseo

THE MARKS OF SAINT PETER'S KNEES

Prayer to interrupt the levitation of a sorcerer

Two stone slabs, worn down in the centre, are ensconced in the right wall of the transept of the church dedicated to Saint Frances of Rome (previously to Santa Maria Nuova), as you can see by ascending the two flights of stairs by the side of the crypt.
Tradition holds that these are the imprints left by Saint Peter's knees (or Saint Peter's and Saint Paul's, according to some sources) while praying to God to intervene against Simon Magus, who had levitated himself in the space above the Forum to show his superiority over the two Apostles. The prayer proved effective as the heretic fell to the ground and died on the spot.
Documents bearing witness to the life of Simon Magus have rarely been officially recognised, as the texts do not always agree and are largely derived from apocryphal sources, but according to the most popular version Simon was a magician or sorcerer from a small village in Samaria. On hearing Christian teaching, he requested baptism, although that did not stop him trying to bribe Saint Peter – who took it very badly – in order to acquire the privilege of transmitting the Holy Spirit by the laying on of hands.

It was precisely this legendary attempt by Simon Magus to commercialise spiritual gifts that gave rise to the term *simony*.

BLESSING MOTORISTS

Every year on 9 March, a vast number of the faithful gather in their cars in Via dei Fori Imperiali and Piazza del Colosseo, trying their best to park as near to the church as possible to receive the solemn blessing bestowed in the name of Saint Frances of Rome.
This rich and noble lady lived in Rome until her death in 1440. She owed her fame to her generosity, having devoted her life to helping the poor and the sick. In 1425 she founded the Oblate Congregation of Tor de' Specchi. She was declared a saint in 1608 and made patron saint of motorists in 1925.

IN QVESTE
PIETRE POSE
LE GINOCHIA S·PIETRO
QVANDO I DEMONII PORT·
SIMON MAGO
PER ARIA

03.

Via dei Cerchi, 87
Metro B – Circo Massimo

THE HAND ON VIA DEI CERCHI

The hand of Cicero

Along Via dei Cerchi, a narrow street that winds between the Circus Maximus and the Palatine Hill, stands a building whose architecture is strikingly original: above the cornice, which features 18 large oculi, a strange hand crowns the construction.

This hand is a plaster copy – on a smaller scale – of a Roman marble original that was found in the area and originally featured on the façade of the little church of the Madonna dei Cerchi, also known as Santa Maria de Manu, built in the 13th century and demolished in 1939. The thumb and forefinger of the hand point towards the sky. In ancient Rome, from the days of the Republic, this gesture had a precise meaning: it was how military commanders and emperors demanded silence before the *adlocutio*, a speech to rouse the troops before battle.

Popular tradition refers to this sculpture as the 'hand of Cicero', although there is no reason to associate it with the famous Roman orator.

Inside the building, the windows are surrounded with decorative motifs, notably the fleur-de-lys, heraldic symbol of the Farnese family. The site is in fact at the foot of the Orti Farnesiani (Farnese gardens), which Cardinal Alessandro Farnese ordered to be planted from 1520. In this northern section of the Palatine Hill, the first private botanical gardens in Europe were created; they were inherited by the Bourbons of Naples and subsequently sold to Napoleon III, before the Italian government acquired them after unification in 1870.

The building must originally have been one of the farmhouses on the extensive Farnese estate, but it was embellished with this complex façade during renovations at the end of the 17th century. It is now part of the properties of the Olivetan Benedictine monks, who own the basilica of Sant'Anastasia, whose apse lies behind this building.

At the time of Sixtus V (1585–1590), the common people believed that the hand indicated the price of wine: 1 sou per fojetta (half a litre).

04.

Piazza della Bocca della Verità, 16
Metro B – Circo Massimo; Bus 51, 81, 85, 87 – Cerchi/Bocca della Verità

THE MITHRAIC SANCTUARY OF CIRCO MASSIMO

One of the largest Mithraic sanctuaries in Rome

In the early 1930s, during restoration work on the building facing the north-west of the Circo Massimo (Circus Maximus), at a depth of 14 metres below the present road level, the remains of a vast brick building from the 2nd century CE were discovered.

Its location suggested a public building related to the neighbouring circus. This hypothesis is confirmed by the presence of a majestic flight of steps, a later addition leading to an upper storey.

In the 3rd century CE, certain ground-floor rooms were converted to house one of the largest Mithraic sanctuaries known in Rome. Access is by a secondary entrance and a passage to the right, from which opens a service chamber.

A wide brick archway separates this chamber from the sanctuary proper, the sides of which are fitted with raised stone benches for use by worshippers. On the rear wall, a semi-circular niche probably held a statue of the god.

The floor is paved with blocks of salvaged marble while in the centre of the sanctuary stands a circular alabaster stone remarkable for its size.

The scene is completed by an incredible white marble relief showing Mithras in the act of slaying a bull, surrounded by his two torch-bearers (*dadofori*) Cautes and Cautopates, the Sun, the Moon, a raven, a scorpion, a dog and a serpent.

WHY IS THERE A TOWER WITHIN THE CIRCUS MAXIMUS?

The medieval Torre della Moletta (Tower of the Little Mill) was part of a fortified complex that belonged to the Frangipane family, a powerful Roman clan. It is so called because of a nearby water mill, powered by the Aqua Mariana channel that flowed right through the centre of the circus.

OTHER MITHRAIC SANCTUARIES IN ROME

– The *sanctuary of Santa Prisca* has some important paintings, a splendid effigy of the Sun god in opus sectile (composed of fragments of marble), and in a niche in the rear wall, the image of Mithras, unusually depicted naked, slaying the bull. An additional bonus is a reclining image of the god Saturn made with fragments of amphorae covered with stucco.

– The *sanctuary of San Clemente* is located on the lowest level of the crypt of the church of the same name. The chamber is small in size and equipped with a central altar carved on all four sides. The vault, decorated with stucco stars, is pierced with 11 apertures: the largest, circular ones probably represent the seven planets of the solar system that were known at the time and which were associated with the seven grades of initiation, while four smaller rectangular openings feature the four seasons. At the back of the chamber, a niche houses a small statue of Mithras springing from the rock at his birth.

– The *sanctuary of the Palazzo Barberini* park is unique because it features ten small paintings illustrating key episodes in the life of Mithras. These pictures frame a large painting of the tauroctony and the 12 signs of the zodiac.

– The *sanctuary of the Baths of Caracalla* is the largest known in Rome. Roofed by large barrel vaults, the main chamber measures 23 by 10 metres. In the centre is a pit where an underground passage ends. This was thought to have been the fossa sanguinis of the sanctuary – the place where the initiate would lie prostrate during the ceremony in order to be doused with blood from the bull sacrificed in the hall overhead. This hypothesis seems dubious, however, given the practical difficulties of sacrificing such a large animal in these cramped and difficult to access caverns. This Mithraic sanctuary has retained its paving of white mosaic with a border of black tiles.

– The *sanctuary of the crypt of the church of Santo Stefano Rotondo* is still decorated with a few frescoes of the Sun and Moon.

– The *sanctuary of Via Giovanni Lanza* measures less than 6 square metres. Probably a site for private use, it was miraculously intact when discovered. The relief ornamentation, altar, oil lamps and antique vases were even in their original places.

MITHRAISM – A FASCINATING ANCIENT CULT FOR INITIATES

Mithraism is a religion centred on Mithras, a god of Persian origin. Mithras was born naked, springing from the living rock armed with a knife, a flaming torch in his hand, and a Phrygian cap on his head. A pact was signed after Mithras defeated the Sun. He thereby received the Sun's radiant crown, which became his emblem. In his tireless struggle against evil, with the help of his dog he captured and killed a bull, symbol of the impetuous animal forces that must be overcome. Grain miraculously spilled from the bull's wound, while its blood became the grapevine. Its death thus allowed rebirth. The evil spirit Ahriman, however, refused to admit defeat: he sent a scorpion and a serpent to attack Mithras, but to no avail. Mithras and the Sun then held a celebratory ritual meal known as an agape, a term still current today. The cult of Mithras was usually celebrated in caves and grottoes, not because of any link with the powers of darkness, as some detractors would have it, but rather because the cave was a symbol of the cosmos, towards which believers tried to reach out during the ceremonies. Mithras was flanked by two torch-bearers: Cautes and Cautopates, with whom he formed a triad (or Trinity). The first carried a lighted torch which represented the day, while the second carried an extinguished torch, pointing downwards, symbol of the night. The concept of the soul's journey across the cosmos is key to all this: the way consisted of seven steps, linked to the seven planets, the seven days of the week, the seven metals and the seven stages of the soul which had to be gradually left behind. The cult was clearly a means of advancing on this path and progressively freeing oneself from passion. The agape feast, based on bread and wine, of course recalls the Eucharist, and the sacrifice of the bull from which life sprang is a strange reminder of the crucifixion and resurrection. Mithraism spread to the West from the 1st century BCE and was at its peak in the 3rd century CE, before being supplanted by Christianity.

CHRISTMAS OWES 25 DECEMBER TO THE WINTER SOLSTICE AND MITHRAISM ...

Contrary to widespread belief, no Christian scriptures actually claim that Jesus was born on the night of 24 to 25 December. The date of 25 December for Christ's birth was decreed in 354 CE by Pope Liberius to combat pagan Roman cults, and above all, Mithraism, which celebrated the birth of its god Mithras on 25 December to roughly coincide with the winter solstice (prior to the Gregorian reform of the calendar, the winter solstice was not fixed and did not always fall on 21 December – which incidentally was one reason for the reform). The appropriation of this date by the Church also allowed some very beautiful symbolism to develop: at the time of year when the days were shortest and night reigned supreme, the birth of Christ was a powerful symbol of day breaking once again, chasing away the shadows and heralding the resurrection. Previously, Christians celebrated the birth of Christ on 6 January, the day of the Adoration of the Magi. Only the Armenian Apostolic Church still celebrates Christmas on that date. Orthodox faiths continue to commemorate Christmas on 25 December, but according to the Julian calendar, which differs by several days from the reformed Gregorian version. Note also that Jesus was probably not born in 1 CE, but sometime between 6 BCE and 6 CE.

05.

Piazza di San Gregorio
Metro B – Circo Massimo

THE TABLE OF SANTA BARBARA ORATORY

Here Saint Gregory fed twelve paupers – and an angel joined them as the thirteenth guest

The surrounding wall of the splendid staircase leading to the church of San Gregorio al Celio is interrupted halfway up, on the left, by a gateway. You only need to go through this and ascend a few more steps to reach the site of three buildings: the oratories of Santa Barbara, Sant'Andrea and Santa Silvia.

It is said that the Barbara oratory was the former residence of Pope Saint Gregory I (Gregory the Great, 590–604) and that the sovereign pontiff had installed therein a large marble table on which he offered a daily meal to 12 paupers.

One day, a thirteenth guest was present at the table – an angel who had taken on the guise of a poor man – and Gregory decided to feed him too. It is tempting to see in this person the figure of the traitor Judas, the thirteenth at the Last Supper, and to interpret Gregory's invitation as a call to love and forgive even those who betray us. Hence began the tradition, which persisted until 1870, to bring together 13 guests at a meal offered by the pope each Holy Thursday, symbolising the pardoning of the traitor. The popular superstition that it is wiser to avoid seating 13 at table is no less active today.

This very old oratory includes the ruins of a 3rd-century Roman building. It was restored on the initiative of Cardinal Baronio between 1602 and 1603. A marble statue representing Saint Gregory the Great bestowing a blessing, the work of Nicolas Cordier, stands in a niche. The walls are decorated with a series of frescoes attributed to Antonio Viviani carried out in 1603 and 1604, with scenes from the life of the pontiff.

The most striking object, in the centre of the chamber, is of course the large table, the very one where the 12 paupers ate. This massive structure in white marble, supported by two large stone griffons with a central palm tree, dates from the 3rd century CE. An inscription recalling the miracle of the angel reads: *Bissenos hoc Gregorius pascebat egentes – Angelus et decimus tertius accubuit* (Here Saint Gregory fed 12 paupers – and an angel joined them as the thirteenth guest).

06.

Church of Santo Stefano Rotondo
Via di Santo Stefano Rotondo, 7
Metro B – Colosseo; Bus 3 – Colosseo

X-RATED FRESCOES IN ST STEPHEN'S

The spectre of death in a foreign land ...

In 1580, Pope Gregory XIII handed over the church of Santo Stefano al Celio to the Jesuits of the Collegium Germanicum et Hungaricum, where clergymen were trained for the evangelisation of northern and central Europe. After 1517, many inhabitants of these regions had joined Luther's Protestant Reformation. The Roman Catholic Church therefore decided – after the Council of Trent (1545–1563) – to save their souls by sending young Jesuits to proselytise among them.
To accustom young priests to the idea that they might die on this mission, the Jesuits of the Collegium Germanicum commissioned a series of murals for the walls of the circular nave. This resulted in 34 scenes of martyrdom by famous painters of the time, including Niccolò Pomarancio and Antonio Tempesta. These terrifyingly graphic paintings can still be seen today. The artists were perhaps inspired by the writings of Antonio Gallonio, a priest of the same period – known for his biography of Saint Philip Neri – who in one of his works, illustrated by Tempesta himself, had described in great detail the martyrdom of early Christians.

The church of Santo Stefano Rotondo (Saint Stephen in the Round) on the Celian Hill, dating from the 5th century, seems to have taken its central plan from Eastern architecture. At the centre was a drum, 22 metres high and 22 metres in diameter, lit by 22 windows and supported by 22 columns. Around this nucleus ran two circular naves, with ambulatories and other architectural features. At the time of Pope Theodore I (642–649), the relics of the martyrs Primus and Felicianus were placed in one of the original chapels. This, in addition to the beautiful mosaic in the apse depicting the two martyrs, is the only chapel to have survived the ravages of time.
Over the centuries, the outer circular nave was destroyed, so that the inner nave has come to form the perimeter wall of the church.

D
B
C
E
A

07.

Santi Quattro Coronati Basilica
Via dei Santi Quattro Coronati
Metro B – Colosseo

GAME IN THE CLOISTER OF SANTI QUATTRO CORONATI BASILICA

Ancient game or measuring rod?

The basilica of Santi Quattro Coronati, although little known to the public, is one of the most charming and romantic religious buildings in Rome. The cloister, founded in the 13th century, is a marvel of beauty, sweetness and light, accentuated by the second-floor gallery and the double columns supporting it.

Just at the entrance to the cloister, on a low wall set between two rows of columns, 15 parallel lines are carved into the stone, in the middle of which can be read signs that might be interpreted as Roman numerals. Some have seen this as a measuring rod or abacus from antiquity, others believe it was an ancient game resembling either snakes and ladders or dice, in which the number of points won depended on the distance from the two columns.

Almost opposite these lines on the other side of the cloister, there are more inscriptions, also subject to various interpretations. Two of these – the Nine Men's Morris and the esoteric symbol of the triple enclosure – have their supporters. The same inscription is found carved a second time on the wall of the cloister itself but has been almost obliterated.

For more information on triple enclosures, see page 214.

08.

Piazza di San Clemente
Metro B – Colosseo

VERBAL ABUSE IN BASILICA SAN CLEMENTE

Sons of whores, pull harder!

In the Lower Basilica of San Clemente, the 11th-century frescoes showing Saint Clement celebrating Mass reveal a little-known episode in the life of the saint (bottom right of the fresco).

The Roman prefect Sisinnius's wife Theodora, who had been converted to Christianity by Saint Clement, was beginning to spend a great deal of her time at church. Her husband, suspicious of her new faith, took her frequent absences as signs of infidelity and decided to follow her to find out what was going on, although she was simply attending Mass.

During the service, however, divine intervention struck down the jealous husband, rendering him deaf and blind.

Theodora implored Saint Clement to heal her husband and the saint, praying to God, did so, but Sisinnius then got it into his head that the saint was a magician who had bewitched his wife in order to take advantage of her. So he ordered his servants to seize Clement and carry him away.

For the second time a miracle occurred: the servants, believing they had trussed up the saint, found that they had only managed to tie their ropes around a stout column. The fresco describes the exact moment when the exasperated Sisinnius, right, dressed in a toga, cries: '*Fili de le pute, traite!*' ['Pull harder, you sons of whores!'] – the terms of abuse are clearly visible on the fresco. One of the servants, Gosmari, repeats the order to another, Albertel: 'Albertel, traite', who in turn asks a third fellow for help: 'Falite dereto co lo palo, Carvoncelle' ['Carvoncelle, get behind with a lever'] – the inscription can still be seen bottom left.

Meanwhile, Clement, safely out of the way, comments on the scene in learned Latin: '*Duritiam cordis vestri saxa trahere meruisti*' ['You deserve to carry a great burden given the hardness of your hearts'].

THE LEGEND OF POPE JOAN

In an oratory at the junction of Via dei Santi Quattro and Via dei Querceti there is a painting in very poor condition that has often been interpreted as a memorial of the scandal of the legendary Pope Joan, who gave birth in the street. In fact it is simply a Virgin and Child.

The anti-papal satire of Pope Joan probably originated in popular culture during the 9th century and enjoyed great success in 13th and 14th-century court circles, although largely forgotten today.

It is said that on the death of Pope Leo IV, a young man from the German city of Mainz was elected pope under the title of John VIII and supposedly reigned from 853 to 855 (the pontificate of Leo IV in fact lasted until his death in 855, and Benedict III succeeded him a few weeks later). The young man in question was really a young girl who had just arrived in Rome disguised as a man, after studying in Athens. As she excelled in literary and scientific argument, she gained the respect of a number of academics. Still dressed in male attire, she quickly surrounded herself with followers and became so celebrated that she was made pope. Struggling with great difficulty against her natural desires, however, the young woman grew infatuated with a handsome cardinal, who at first was annoyed by the way she was looking at him. But his irritation melted as soon as he realised that the pope was really a young and beautiful Papessa. The two clerics wasted no time in becoming lovers and, uniquely in the history of the Church, the pope fell pregnant.

The story goes on to say that one day, on the processional route between the Lateran and Saint Peter's, the Papessa's waters broke and she gave birth in the middle of the road, near Saint Clement's church. The place is marked with a stone slab and the street, which no longer exists, came to be known as Vico della Papessa. Pope Joan's name does not appear today on the list of holy pontiffs, in an attempt to eradicate the memory of this shameful incident. Moreover, the legend has it that thereafter it was stipulated that during a pope's consecration ceremony two cardinals must verify the sex of the new candidate by seating him on a seat with a hole in it, to check his attributes, and that after verification they should declare: *Habet duos testiculos et bene pendentes* ('He has two well-hung testicles').

But this story was rather discredited by the existence of 'commodes' manufactured long before the election of the Papessa. The Church officially denied the legend in 1570, but it is said that until then the Easter processions carefully avoided the Vico della Papessa. In fact the papal processions never used that street.

09.

Basilica di San Giovanni in Laterano
Piazza di San Giovanni in Laterano, 4
Metro A – San Giovanni

THE TRIPLE ENCLOSURES OF SAN GIOVANNI IN LATERANO CLOISTER

Just a game, or an esoteric symbol?

The superb cloister of San Giovanni in Laterano (Saint John Lateran), designed by Vassalletto in the 13th century, has three curious and discreet inscriptions within its grounds. Just to the right of the entrance is the first of these three markings, which some refer to as 'triple enclosures'. There are two other sets of these interlocking squares in the cloister, this time traced vertically on the outer walls of the cloister. Numerous interpretations of these inscriptions exist (see below).

NINE MEN'S MORRIS OR ESOTERIC SYMBOL?

The same grid, composed of three interlocking squares with four horizontal lines that stop short of the central square, can be found carved in many places in Europe, and even in China and Sri Lanka. Although some see this as just a board game known as Nine Men's Morris, it has been pointed out that this inscription has been found carved on vertical walls or reproduced on a very small scale, which would prevent it from being used as the basis for a game. Thus the grid is also thought to be an esoteric symbol used in spiritual quests, representing the three gradations on an initiate's path from the temporal to the sacred final goal, passing through the three worlds of the physical, intellectual, and spiritual or divine. It could also represent Heavenly Jerusalem with its 12 doors (three on each side of the grid). Used by the Knights Templar to mark sacred geographical sites or places where there was a particular concentration of physical and spiritual energy, the grid is also sometimes found in circular form. The circle initially would have corresponded to the beginning of the road while the square signified the culmination of the quest, hence the expression 'squaring the circle' to symbolise the successful resolution of a problem.

Nine Men's Morris, also known as Mills or Merrills in English, has been played since antiquity (in Rome, Greece and Egypt). Two players each have nine pieces ('men') and take turns placing them on one of the board's 24 intersections. The object of the game is to align three pieces belonging to the same player. Sometimes ordinary pebbles of different colours are used.

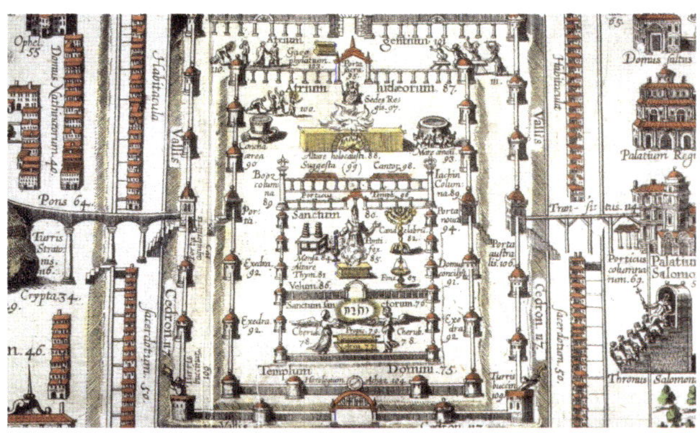

There are four places in Rome where such a grid can be seen: the basilicas of Santi Quattro Coronati, San Giovanni in Laterano, San Paolo Fuori le Mura, and San Lorenzo Fuori le Mura.

10.

Basilica di San Giovanni in Laterano - Sancta Sanctorum
Piazza di San Giovanni in Laterano, 4
Metro A – San Giovanni

THE RELIC OF CHRIST'S FORESKIN

Is the Holy Prepuce at the Lateran?

According to Jewish tradition, Jesus was circumcised eight days after his birth. At a time when Christianity was fighting over the possession of holy relics, a great many far-fetched artefacts saw the light of day (see following double pages), including the foreskin of Christ. This is very likely to be one of the many faked relics and moreover one that is not recognised by the Church. At Coulombs Abbey in France, a local belief attributes the holy relic with the power to make barren women fertile and give pregnant women an easy childbirth. This was why Catherine of Valois, the widow of King Henry V of England, had the relic brought to her in 1421 to ensure a successful birth.

In the Middle Ages, there were as many as fifteen different Holy Prepuces in Europe, although the one in Rome was the most renowned. It was said to have been offered as a wedding gift by the Byzantine empress, Irene the Athenian, and placed in the Sancta Santorum of the Lateran by the pope.

Several examples having been destroyed during the French Revolution, three other places of the original fifteen now claim the holy relic: Antwerp in Belgium, Conques and Vebret (Auvergne) in France.

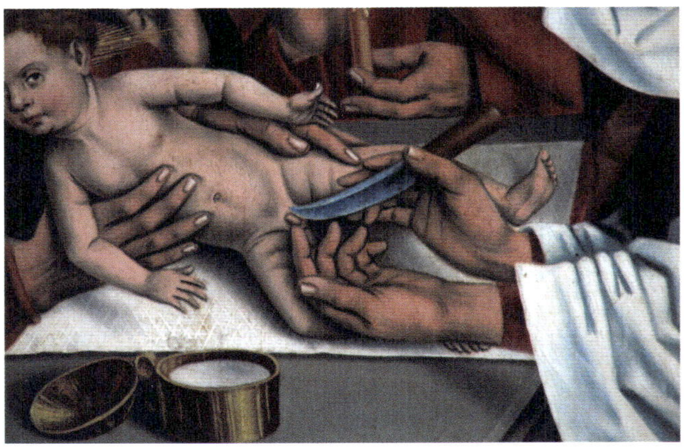

MORE POWERFUL THAN THE HOLY FORESKIN, THE HOLY UMBILICAL CORD OF CHRIST!

At the height of the competition over holy relics (see following double pages), an improbable example was invented by unscrupulous merchants: the Holy Umbilicus, said to be the remains of Jesus' umbilical cord. This relic is preserved today at the church of San Giovanni in Laterano, with another small fragment at Santa Maria del Popolo. Note that another Holy Umbilicus is thought to have existed at Châlons-en-Champagne, in France, until 1707, when the relic was destroyed by the bishop who judged it to be a fake. The town is said to have acquired the relic thanks to Charlemagne who himself received it from the Byzantine emperor. He was supposed to have given it to one of the popes, whose successor passed on a fragment to the bishop of Châlons.

THE CULT OF CHRISTIAN RELICS

Although rather neglected these days, with their devoted following greatly diminished in numbers, saints' relics had extraordinary success from the Middle Ages onwards. Their presence today in numerous churches across Europe is a reminder of those exceptional times.

The cult of Christian relics goes back to the beginning of Christianity, to the deaths of the early martyrs and the creation of the first saints.

The function of these relics was threefold: they bore witness to the example of a righteous and virtuous life to be copied or followed; they possessed a spiritual energy and power that could even work miracles (it was believed that the miraculous powers of the saints themselves were retained by their relics); and over time, with the rise of the contested practice of granting indulgences, relics bestowed indulgences on those who possessed them (see opposite).

As demand dictated supply, it was not long before unscrupulous parties were competing to invent their own relics, aided in their task by the Church which, for political reasons, canonised a great number of undeserving individuals (see opposite). Overproduction went to absurd extremes: if the authenticity of all their relics was to be accepted, Mary Magdalene would have had six bodies, and St Biagio a hundred arms.

These excesses, of course, raised suspicions and the popularity of relics gradually waned, although many people still believe that the true relic of a saint possesses spiritual power. How else can the numerous pilgrimages in the footsteps of Padre Pio throughout Italy be explained?

There are around 50,000 relics scattered around Europe, from some 5,000 saints.

Note that most of the world's other religions also worship relics, or used to do so.

21,441 RELICS FOR 39,924,120 YEARS OF INDULGENCES!

The greatest collector of relics was Frederick III of Saxony (1463–1525), who procured 21,441 of them in all, 42 of which were fully preserved bodies of saints. Based on this unique collection, he calculated that he had amassed a grand total of 39,924,120 years and 220 days of indulgences! However, under the influence of Luther, who opposed indulgences, he abandoned the cult of relics in 1523.

WHEN SAINTS ARE NOT SO HOLY

From the Middle Ages onwards, the pursuit of relics continued, as did their falsification. Not only relics were fabricated, however. Sometimes, even the saints themselves were a fabrication. Recently – an event that passed almost without comment – the Church purged St. George, St. Christopher and St. Philomena from its calendar, the very existence of all three now being in doubt. The totally abusive canonisation of certain real personalities also took place, allowing the objects connected with them to feed the market for saintly relics. For diplomatic reasons linked to the Counter-Reformation of the 16th century, canonisation was often based on political rather than religious or moral criteria. As a result of this Realpolitik, many rulers of the time were thus sanctified in a bid to ensure their subjects' allegiance to the Roman Catholic Church, then under pressure from the Protestant movement. St. Stanislas of Poland, St. Casimir of Lithuania, St. Brigitte of Sweden, St. Stephen of Hungary, St. Margaret of Scotland, St. Elizabeth of Portugal, St. Wenceslas of Bohemia ... The list is long, indeed.

PHANTASMAGORICAL RELICS

Leaving no stone unturned in their efforts to make money at the expense of the most naive believers, relic merchants showed unparalleled imagination in their quest for sacred paraphernalia and invented some fascinating objects, such as the horns of Moses or the feathers of the Archangel Michael, recorded as having been on sale at Mont-Saint-Michel in 1784. The most highly prized relics were of course those of Christ. Unfortunately for relic hunters, as Christ had ascended to Heaven, his body was by definition no longer on Earth. Imagination again came to the rescue in the form of the quite extraordinary relic of the breath of Jesus (!) which was preserved in Wittenberg cathedral, Germany, in a glass phial. The remains of Christ's foreskin, recuperated after his circumcision seven days after birth, and of his umbilical cord (!) were preserved at Lateran, Rome (in the Sancta Sanctorum) while bread from the Last Supper was kept at Gaming, Austria. Certain medieval texts lost to us today even spoke of the relic of the rays of the star that guided the Wise Men, also preserved at Lateran.

11.

Piazzale Labicano
Tram 5, 14 – Piazza di Porta Maggiore; Bus 7 – Piazza di Porta Maggiore

THE BAKER'S TOMB

An imperial tomb for a simple baker

Virtually an imperial monument, the monument to Marco Virgilio Eurisace is just the tomb of an ordinary baker. It was rediscovered in the late 19th century when Pope Gregory XVI demolished the defensive towers that Honorius had built beside the Porta Maggiore in 1838, in order to restore the site to the aspect it enjoyed in the Aurelian era. Constructed from concrete and travertine in 30 BCE, the monument curiously resembles the patrician tombs of the Appian Way.
As the inscription points out: *Est hoc monimentum Marcei Vergilei Eurysacis pistoris, redemptoris, apparet* ('This is the tomb of Marcus Vergilius Eurysaces, baker, contractor, provisioning breadmaker').
The man, who was a subordinate (*apparitore*) to a high-ranking figure, was probably an emancipated slave who worked for the state.
On the tomb are a number of symbols of the baker's trade.
The tomb itself is shaped like the vessel in which he would have kneaded the bread. It is decorated with numerous bas-reliefs representing the utensils used to make bread, as well as the production process itself: weighing the wheat, sifting the flour, preparing the dough, placing the bread in the oven …
The urn in which the ashes of his wife Atinia are preserved, now in the Museo delle Terme in Rome, was made in the form of a dough trough.
Finally, the bas-relief depicting two spouses at the Capitoline Museums probably comes from another, now ruined, section of this monument.

The Museo della Civiltà Romana (Museum of Roman Civilisation), in the EUR district, holds a miniature reproduction of the tomb.

The Porta Maggiore was so named to indicate to pilgrims the route that led to the church of Santa Maria Maggiore.

QUIRINALE – TERMINI – MONTI –

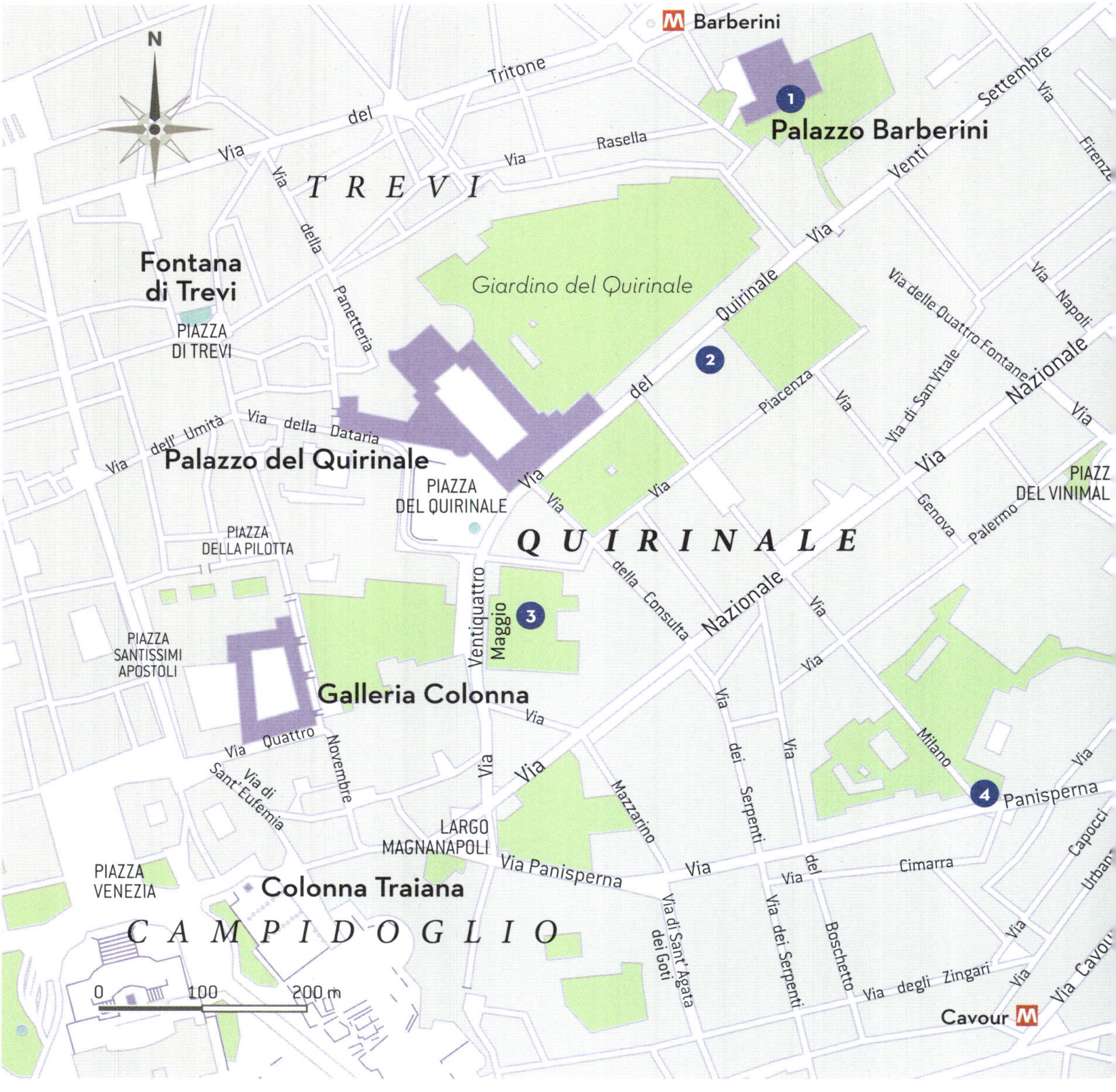

01. *DIVINE WISDOM* FRESCO *p. 224*

02. THE STATUE OF STANISLAS KOSTKA *p. 226*

03. CASINO DELL'AURORA *p. 228*

04. MUSEO DI PATOLOGIA DEL LIBRO *p. 230*

05. ANACHRONISTIC CHARACTERS IN THE SANTA PUDENZIANA MOSAIC *p. 232*

06. THE BUST OF NEGRITA *p. 234*

ESQUILINO

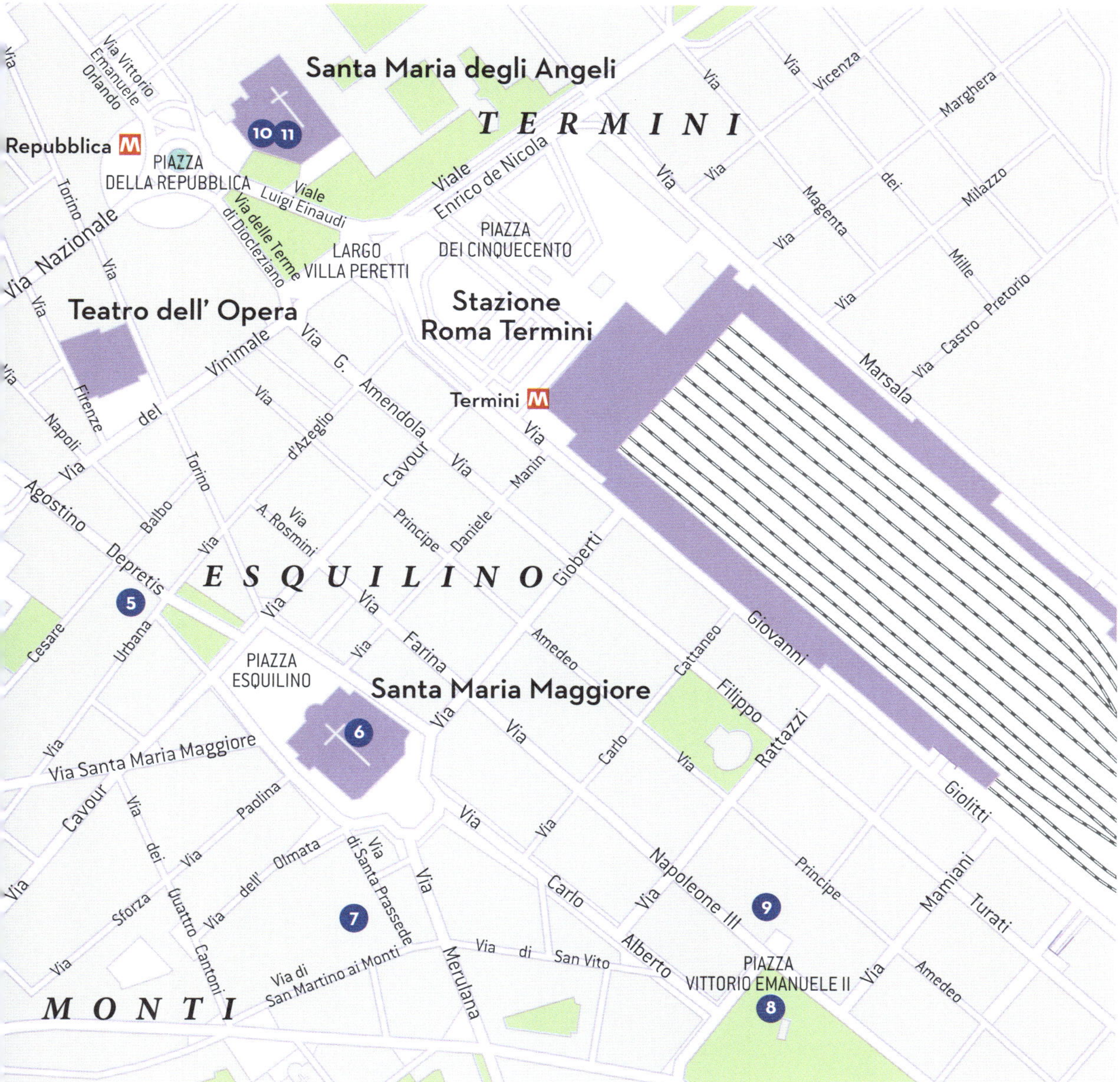

07. THE SQUARE HALO OF SANTA PRASSEDE BASILICA *p. 236*

08. MARQUIS PALOMBARA'S PORTA ALCHEMICA *p. 238*

09. BLESSING OF THE ANIMALS AT SANT'EUSEBIO *p. 242*

10. THE SUNDIAL OF SANTA MARIA DEGLI ANGELI CHURCH *p. 244*

11. THE BOREAL MERIDIAN OF SANTA MARIA DEGLI ANGELI CHURCH *p. 250*

01.

Galleria Nazionale d'Arte Antica - Palazzo Barberini
Via delle Quattro Fontane, 13
Metro A – Barberini

DIVINE WISDOM FRESCO

A mirror of Tommaso Campanella's theocratic

The Allegory of Divine Wisdom in the beautiful Palazzo Barberini was commissioned by Taddeo Barberini (1603–1647), nephew of Pope Urban VIII, from the Italian painter Andrea Sacchi (1599–1661), who masterfully carried out the task between 1629 and 1631-33. Sacchi was a friend and disciple of the philosopher and theologian Tommaso Campanella (1568–1639), a follower of the Gnostic ideas of his time and a supporter of Church reform, which condemned him to many years in prison for heresy and conspiracy. Campanella entered the Dominican Order in his youth. However, in both thought and action, he was a Christian who believed that the pope – as the spiritual leader of Christendom – could establish a state with perfect social justice among countries while ruling from the Vatican, a state where religion and politics were reconciled in perfect harmony: a true papal theocracy. He even wrote a utopian treatise entitled *La città del sole* (The City of the Sun).

According to Campanella, Pope Urban VIII had all the cultural and moral qualities of a truly supreme pontiff. Campanella became an intimate adviser and friend of the Vatican curia and when, in 1634, the Inquisition again tried to arrest him, the pope personally arranged his flight to Paris. Previously, Campanella had immortalised Urban VIII Barberini and affirmed his divine mission on Earth, once risen to papal power, through Sacchi's Divine Wisdom fresco: it represents the famous City of the Sun that Campanella yearned for.

In a 1633 treatise, Campanella had already described his ideal of the universal emperor of a Catholic monarchy, *Monarchia messiae*, an evocative title that reflected the ideas previously expressed in City of God by another Neoplatonic, Saint Augustine.

In Campanella's opinion, the reign of Urban VIII was the realisation on Earth of the City of the Sun. In the fresco, Divine Wisdom is surrounded by the virtues essential to this realisation: Nobility wearing the crown of Ariane, Eternity and the serpent biting its tail forming the circle of infinity, Justice with the scales, Courage with the key of Hercules, Gentleness with a lyre, Divinity with the triangle, Charity with an ear of wheat, Holiness with the cross and the burning altar, Purity with the swan, Insight with the eagle and Beauty with the hair of Berenice.

In the sky appear two winged figures: a man astride a winged lion, an allegory of God's love; and, opposite, Cupid holding an arrow and pointing to a hare that symbolises the fear of God.

Finally, at the feet of Divine Wisdom and in alignment, a huge globe appears to rotate in orbit around the throne. It suggests that Andrea Sacchi knew the heliocentric theory supported by Galileo, but instigated by Copernicus.

HERMETIC FRESCO

Note also in the *Divine Wisdom* fresco the small stars positioned near the painted virtues. They represent the sky on the night of 5 to 6 August 1623, when Urban VIII Barberini was elected pope. Thus, in perfect correspondence with the Hermetic theories of the time (see page 156), this painting was not just decorative but served as a talisman. It was supposed to reproduce and disseminate the conjunctions of the stars favourable to Urban VIII, thus protecting him from the negative influences of Mars and Saturn at the time of solar and lunar eclipses. Urban VIII was a discreet but dedicated believer in astrology and Campanella had even studied the planets that influenced the pope in his work Campanellae Astrologicorum Libri VI, under the title *De siderali fato vitando*.

02.

Church of Sant'Andrea al Quirinale
Via del Quirinale, 30
Metro A – Repubblica; Bus 71, 117 – Milano/Nazionale

THE STATUE OF STANISLAS KOSTKA

A marvellous statue embedded in a picture frame

Most visitors to Sant'Andrea al Quirinale, who restrict themselves to the main church precinct, will not suspect they are missing the best part: at the back of the church a passage to the right leads into a corridor where postcards and other souvenirs are sold.

From there you can enter the two most interesting places in the building, but you need to know about them because they are usually closed. You only have to ask, however, and the door to the superb sacristy will be opened.

This room, with a beautiful richly frescoed ceiling, can be admired with the help of the lamps that will be lit for you, but we recommend investing 50 centesimi in some extra lighting to see it better. For the modest sum of one euro, you can also ask to see the rooms housing the relics of Saint Stanislas Kostka on the first floor of the building (home of the Jesuit seminary). Born in Poland in 1550 and dead by the age of 18 in 1568, Stanislas Kostka entered the Jesuits' novitiate in Rome when he was 16, after studying in Vienna. Against the wishes of his father, he had run away from home in 1567 and crossed the whole of Germany on foot.

In the second room is a quite extraordinary and neglected sculpture by Pierre Legros the Younger, dating from 1702 to 1703. In spectacular detail, it shows the saint lying on his deathbed in a superb blend of polychrome marble that captures the smallest folds in the draperies.

The black marble tunic he is wearing is incredible enough: more like a 19th-century dandy's coat than a religious habit, it means that the saint had not yet been ordained a priest.

You will also notice the curious detail that a section from the painting behind the marble bed has been cut out. This work by Tommaso Minardi depicting the Holy Virgin, Saint Barbara, Saint Cecilia and Saint Agnes welcoming the saint, was hung after the Legros sculpture was in place. As the statue touched the wall, a section of the frame had to be removed to fit in the painting, which is of little interest in itself.

03.

Via XXIV Maggio, 43
Metro B – Cavour; Bus 40, 60, 64, 70 – Nazionale/Quirinale

CASINO DELL'AURORA

See the dawn once a month

In the grounds of the extraordinary Palazzo Pallavicini-Rospigliosi, the Casino dell'Aurora (Dawn Pavilion) is open to the public free of charge on the first day of every month. The palace, built in 1610 over the ruins of the Baths of Constantine, was the former home of the powerful Cardinal Mazarin (Giulio Mazzarino). The *casino* (pavilion), designed at the same time as the hanging garden and the semicircular fountain on the opposite side, was built by the Flemish cabinet-maker Giovanni Vasanzio (the Italian name of Jan Van Santen), who became the assistant of the celebrated architect Flaminio Ponzio upon arriving in Rome. The building's two levels are only visible on the outside from Via XXIV Maggio, because on the other side, which faces the garden, the lower level is buried due to the difference in height between street and garden. The building, which on both levels consists of a central hall flanked by two smaller rooms, has the typical 'C' form of hunting lodges and suburban villas built from the end of the 15th century, and the garden side corresponds to the second floor of the building reserved for banquets and formal ceremonies. On the ceiling of the central hall is the fresco masterpiece that gives the pavilion its name: Aurora by Guido Reni, painted 1613–1614, and one of the most copied works in the history of art over the past four centuries. The central hall is filled with 17th-century marble busts of Roman emperors and famous Greek statues, such as *Artemis the Huntress* and the *Rospigliosi Athena*.

PRIVATE VISIT: THE SIDE ROOMS OF THE CASINO DELL'AURORA

By booking, not only can you visit the pavilion in peace but also gain access to two side rooms that are closed during the monthly public tours. The ceilings are frescoed with Giovanni Baglione's Renaldo and Armida and Passignano's *Battle of Armida*. There are also two paintings by Guido Reni, *Christ Crucified* and *Andromeda Freed by Perseus*, as well as *The Death of Julian the Apostate* and *The Conversion of Saul* by Luca Giordano.

PAVILION OF THE MUSES

Exceptionally it may also be possible to visit the Pavilion of the Muses, which forms part of the same palace complex. Some very fine frescoes can be seen there by Orazio Gentileschi and Agostino Tassi.

PALLAVICINI
PALLAVICINI

04.

Via Milano, 76
Metro B – Cavour; Bus 71, 117 – Milano

MUSEO DI PATOLOGIA DEL LIBRO

Books may suffer, but they will be well looked after

The little-known Museum of Book Pathology was set up in 1938 on the initiative of the Museo dell'Istituto Centrale di Patologia del Libro (Central Institute for Book Pathology). Since then, it has assiduously built up a collection illustrating how books are manufactured and how they eventually deteriorate.
The museum has now been completely refurbished on a new site. A particular attempt has been made to promote a collection of one-of-a-kind objects through a tour laid out in three sections. The first section is devoted to the production materials and techniques of both ancient and modern books. The second covers the various ways in which books can be damaged, and the third their conservation and restoration. Thanks to the experience acquired by the museum staff and the collaboration of the Institute's laboratories, it has been possible to make new teaching aids available to the public that actively encourage visitor participation, making the tour much more interesting for adults as well as for children.
The average length of the museum visit is around 45 minutes. Audio guides in Italian or English are available for all age groups. A series of panels provide a short introduction to each section, while a video illustrates the work of the Institute.
There is also an educational workshop entirely devoted to younger children.

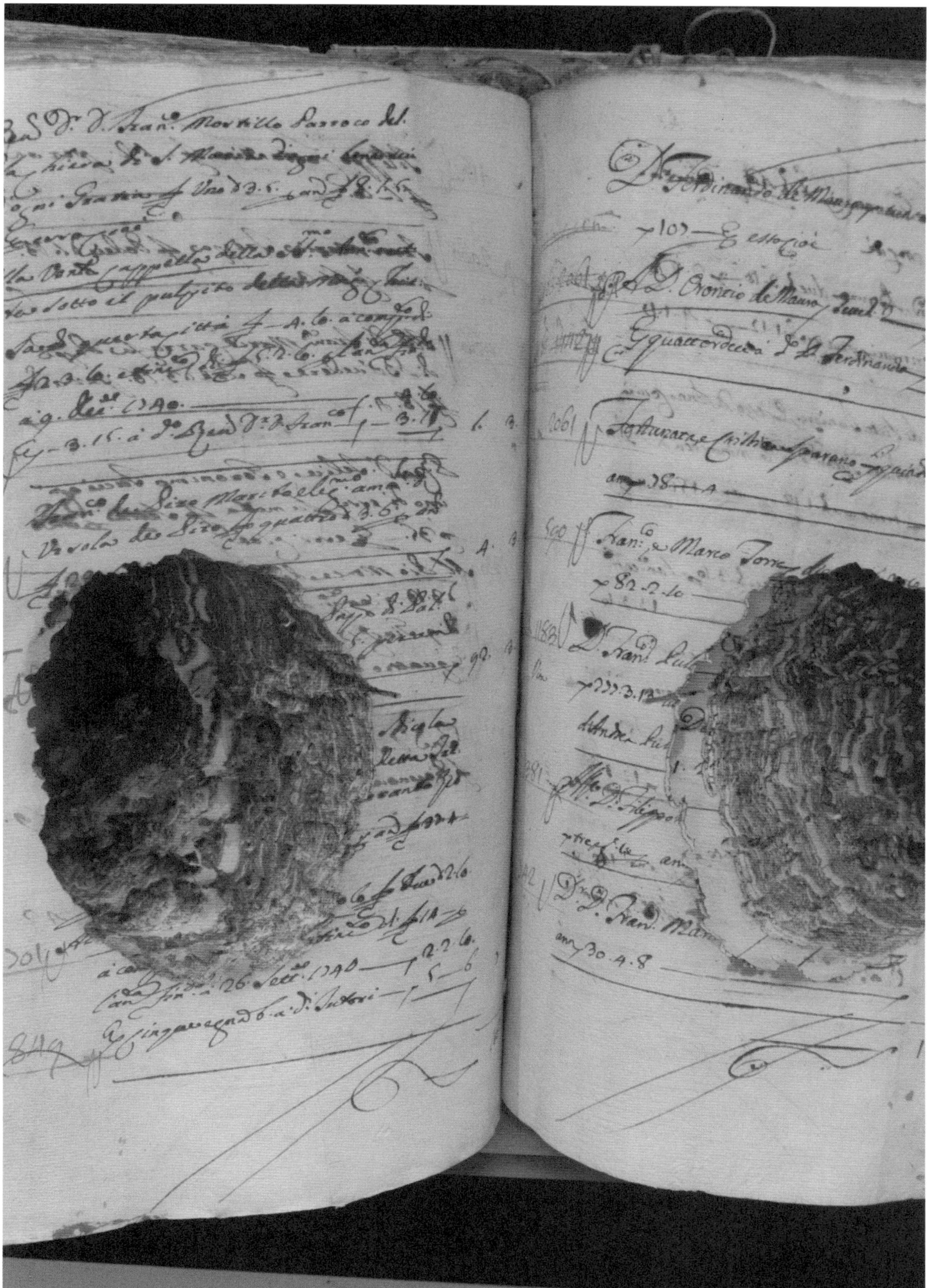

05.

Church of Santa Pudenziana
Via Urbana, 160
Metro A, B – Termini; Bus 70, 7 – arrêt Esquilino/Cavour

ANACHRONISTIC CHARACTERS IN THE SANTA PUDENZIANA MOSAIC

Farnese and Caetani faces in place of those of Christ and the apostles?

Surprisingly, the faces of some figures in the ancient mosaic of the church of Santa Pudenziana are identical to those of famous people of the 16th century, immortalised by great artists.

The face of the second apostle next to Jesus thus bears a disturbing resemblance to Titian's portrait of Pope Paul III (Alessandro Farnese, 1468–1549), while the face of the fourth apostle is very like that of Giulia Farnese – Paul III's sister – shown as the 'Lady and the Unicorn' in several Roman frescoes (Carracci gallery in Palazzo Farnese, Perseus room in Castel Sant'Angelo).

Coincidence? Surely not. The explanation lies in the kinship between Cardinal Enrico Caetani and the Farnese family – Alessandro Farnese's mother was Giovannella Caetani. The relationship between the two families was always very close, to the point that Paul III personally attended the wedding of his cousin, Camillo Caetani, grandfather of the Cardinal Caetani who restored the church in 1585.

The ancient church of Santa Pudenziana (late 4th century) stands beside an old Roman road – *vicus Patricius* – now known as Via Urbana. The church was built on the site of a *domus ecclesiae* known in the 2nd century as Titulus Pudentis. Over the years, the name Pudente was corrupted to Pudenziana and thus at the end of the 4th century the place was already known as Titulus Pudentianae. Popes Siricius and Innocent I (early 5th century) converted parts of the domus into a church. The mosaic of the apsidal arch (dating from 412) is the oldest known among Rome's Christian buildings.

In 1588, Cardinal Enrico Caetani – incumbent of Santa Pudenziana – entrusted the architect Francesco Capriani with the renovation of the church and restoration of the mosaic. Over the centuries, the tesserae that made up the six figures on the right (viewed from a low angle) had all but disappeared. The 16th-century restorer therefore replaced them with 'engraved rendering'. Over the following centuries the mosaic was restored several times: in 1831, during the renovation works of Vincenzo Camuccini, the 16th-century plaster additions were removed and replaced with new tesserae, which nevertheless respected the 'Farnese likenesses'.

06.

Basilica di Santa Maria Maggiore
Piazza di Santa Maria Maggiore
Metro A – Vittorio Emanuele or Termini; Metro B – Termini

THE BUST OF NEGRITA

The remarkable story of the first ambassador from Africa to Europe who died in Rome in the arms of Pope Paul V Borghese in 1604

In the first chapel on the right in the Basilica of Santa Maria Maggiore, a striking black marble bust adorns a Baroque monument. This work, crafted by sculptors Stefano Maderno and Francesco Caporale, is believed to enshrine the remains of Nsaku Ne Vunda (1575–1608), a young ambassador from the Kingdom of Kongo. Baptised and consecrated as a priest with the name António Emmanuele, he was nicknamed 'Negrita' by Europeans due to his dark skin.

The bust stands as a testament to the first formal diplomatic contact between Sub-Saharan Africa and Europe in the modern era. Nsaku Ne Vunda was a relative of King Álvaro II (1578–1614), ruler of a vast Central African empire encompassing present-day Angola, Gabon, and numerous vassal states. An educated man fluent in Latin, Ne Vunda was sent in 1604, at the age of 29, on a mission to Rome.

The goal was to establish direct diplomatic relations with the Holy See, assert Kongo's autonomy from Portuguese influence in ecclesiastical and political affairs, and denounce the slave trade imposed by colonial powers.

Ne Vunda's journey was plagued by obstacles and delays orchestrated by Portugal to thwart his mission. He departed from Mbanza Kongo (modern-day Angola) in 1604 aboard a slave ship bound for Brazil, accompanied by court nobles and family members. Enduring mistreatment on the voyage, he also faced storms and attacks by Dutch pirates before finally arriving on the Iberian Peninsula. In Spain, King Philip III (1578–1621) detained him, further delaying the mission's success. Despite these challenges, Ne Vunda reached Rome on 2 January 1608, gravely ill and with only four companions left.

Pope Paul V Borghese (1552–1621) warmly received him in the Vatican, providing medical care. Tragically, Ne Vunda succumbed to illness just days later, on 6 January 1608, the Feast of the Epiphany. It is said that he died in the Pope's arms. Moved by the young ambassador's story, the Pope ordered a grand funeral procession from the Vatican to the Basilica of Santa Maria Maggiore, where solemn rites were held. He also commissioned the black marble bust, modelled on Ne Vunda's death mask, to preserve his memory.

Ne Vunda's story left a profound impression on Roman society. He was later depicted posthumously, alongside other ambassadors of the era, in the *Salone dei Corazzieri* at the Quirinal Palace. A more intimate portrayal appears in an inaccessible fresco by Giovanni Battista Ricci (1610) in the Pauline Chapel of the Vatican. Pope Paul V Borghese also minted a commemorative medal in his honour.

07.

Santa Prassede Basilica
Via di Santa Prassede, 9
Metro A – Vittorio Emmanuele; Metro B – Cavour

THE SQUARE HALO OF SANTA PRASSEDE BASILICA

Square halos were for subjects alive at the time a mosaic was created

Santa Prassede Basilica, famous for its mosaic cycles made by Byzantine artists in the 9th century, was erected by command of Pope Paschal I (817–824) in honour of Saint Praxedes, the sister of Saint Pudentiana and daughter of Saint Pudens, with whom Saint Peter is said to have stayed. She is also mentioned in the Epistles of St Paul.

The celebrated mosaic in the apse depicts Saints Praxedes and Pudentiana ascending to heaven. To the right of Jesus, Praxedes stands between Saint Zeno and Pope Paschal I, who is presenting Christ with a model of the church he had had built. You will notice that his head is encircled by a very unusual halo: square and blue, instead of the traditional round golden halo (see opposite). Similarly, Paschal's mother Theodora, who is buried in the Saint Zeno chapel, is shown above the door on the left, inside the chapel, also wearing a square blue halo. This type of halo can also be seen in the mosaics of the church of Santa Cecilia in Trastevere, again surrounding the head of Paschal I, who was the force behind the rebuilding of this church too.

Outside the Basilica of Saint John Lateran, the apse mosaic of the remains of Leo III's papal dining hall (*Triclinium Leoninum*) also depicts the pope (795–816) with a square halo.

WHY SQUARE HALOS?

Until the 4th century, only Christ wore a halo, the symbol of those who lived as saints and who had been admitted to heaven. From the 9th century, the halo would nevertheless be accepted for all the saints. These were plain round haloes, the circle being a symbol of perfection and eternity, and golden in colour, symbol of divine light. Haloes are often interpreted as representations of the heavenly space (the aura, in more modern terms) that surrounds the saints. It is focused on the head, supposed to be the noblest part of the human body, the seat of the soul.

The square halo that surrounds certain figures in mosaics signifies that the person was alive at the time the mosaic was made. It represents the earth and the four points of the compass. Blue, the colour of the sky, is the most spiritual, the purest and closest to the divine. It symbolises self-detachment and the flight of the soul towards God and thus indicates an intermediate stage on the path to God and the colour gold.

08.

Piazza Vittorio Emanuele II
Metro A – Vittorio Emanuele; Tram 5, 14 – Principe Eugenio/Manzoni

MARQUIS PALOMBARA'S PORTA ALCHEMICA

A hermetic door?

The Porta Alchemica (Alchemical Door, also known as the Magic Portal, Hermetic Door or Gate of Heaven) is an esoteric monument covered with astrological and alchemical symbols interspersed with Latin and Hebrew phrases with equally occult meanings.

Constructed in 1680, according to the date inscribed there, the Alchemical Door is the only survivor of the five gates of the Villa Palombara built by Massimiliano Palombara, marquis of Pietraforte (1614–1680). The villa was demolished in the late 19th century to enlarge the railway station. In 1873, this door was dismantled only to be reinstalled nearby in 1888, in the gardens of what is now Piazza Vittorio, on an old wall of the church of Saint Eusebius. Two statues of the Egyptian god Bes, taken from the Quirinal Palace, were then added (one on each side).

This minor god of ancient Egypt protected the home from evil spirits and was therefore the patron of sleep, fertility and marriage. These attributes, together with his traditional grotesque image, liken him to the god of gnomes known by ancient students of Hermetism as Gob or Gobi.

Above the door, the medallion in which the orb (globe surmounted by a cross) is superimposed on the six-pointed star, commonly known as the 'Star of David', represents the perfect balance in the harmony between Heaven (upright triangle) and Earth (inverted triangle). In the centre of the first circle is another, smaller, cir-

© Mikhail Malykh

cle, shaped like a stylised rose which in association with the cross recalls the esoteric Rosicrucian movement. Around the two circles are the Latin phrases: *Centrum in trigono centri* ('The centre is in the triangle of the centre') and *Tria sunt mirabilia Deus et Homo Mater et Virgo trinus and unus* ('There are three marvels: God and man, mother and virgin, triune and one').

These two phrases refer to the Third Person of the Trinity, the Holy Spirit, whose name is repeated on the lintel above (*Ruach Elohim* in Hebrew), next to the astrological signs of Saturn (left) and Jupiter. These are also configured as symbols of the constellations of Capricorn and Sagittarius, that is the manifestation of God in matter (Saturn) and the recognition by God of matter (Sagittarius).

This is why Sagittarius is traditionally considered the 'superior aspect' of Capricorn, as borne out by the Latin legend below the Hebrew inscription on the lintel: *Horti magici ingressum hespericus custodit draco et sine alcide colchicas delicias non gustasset iason* ('A dragon guards the entrance to the magic garden of the Hesperides [Saturn] and, without Hercules [Hermes or Mercury], Jason would not have tasted the delights of Colchis [Jupiter]').

On the left door jamb are engraved symbols of Mars and Mercury, each with a Latin heading. The fact that the warlike Mars is in juxtaposition with Mercury means that the temperance of the latter balances and calms the impetuosity of the former, traditionally regarded as the planet of war. From the alchemical point of view, this means that iron (Mars) is moulded by the malleable quicksilver (Mercury). Hence the Latin inscription above the sign of Mars: *Quando in tua domo nigri corvi parturient albas columbas tunc vocaberis sapiens* ('When in your house [Mars] black crows [base matter] give birth to white doves [refined matter], then will you be called wise').

Above the sign of Mercury is written: *Qui scit comburere aqua et lavare igne facit de terra caelum et de caelo terram pretiosam* ('He who can burn with water and wash with fire makes a heaven of earth and a precious earth of heaven'), an obvious reference to the 'arrangement' or balance mentioned.

Engraved on the right door jamb are the symbols of Venus and the Moon, as depicted in the sixth house of the Zodiac by graphically inverting the symbol of Mercury. The sixth house is indeed that of Mercury: the feminine aspect is there in exaltation, represented by Venus (heavenly mother) on the Moon (mother of the world).

Above the sign of Venus, the Latin epigraph reads: *Diameter spherae thau circuli crux orbis non orbis prosunt* ('The diameter of the sphere, the tau in the circle, and the cross of the globe bring no joy to the blind'), meaning those blind to spiritual understanding, non-believers in the sacred science.

Above the Kabbalistic symbol of the Moon is written *Si feceris volare terram super caput tuum eius pennis aquas torrentium convertes in petram* ('If you make the earth fly upside down, with its wings you may convert torrential waters to stone'), referring to the action of the spirit of God incarnate in man trying to transform himself and, therefore, to transform nature. This is known as the work of the Holy Spirit.

At the base of the Alchemical Door, in the centre, is the sign of sulphur, terminated by the strongly initiatory emblem of the conjunction of Jupiter–Saturn: Rosicrucian initiates considered this to be a sign of the universal realisation of the presence of Christ on Earth, when Jupiter (spirit) and Saturn (matter) combine in perfect balance, where the spirit (indicated by the alchemical material sulphur) leads the immediate actions. This is the Rosicrucian enlightenment, equivalent to obtaining the Philosopher's Stone.

Alongside, the double Latin epigraph illustrating this symbol refers to the same effect: *Est opus occultum veri sophi aperire terram ut germinet salutem pro populo* ('It is an occult work of true wisdom to open the earth, so that it may generate salvation for the people') and *Filius noster mortuus vivit rex ab igne redit et coniugio gaudet occulto* ('Our dead son lives, returns from the fire a king [of the world], and enjoys occult conjugation [of the spirit with matter, of Jupiter with Saturn]').

Senator Massimiliano Palombara was an alchemy adept as well as a member of the Rosicrucian brotherhood. The medallion over the door, the only vestige from his palace, is the same as the one on the cover of the alchemical text *Aureum Saeculum Redivivum* (The Golden Age Reborn) by Henricus Madatanus (pseudonym of Adrian von Mynsicht, 1603-1638), also a Rosicrucian. The cover of the original edition of this book published in 1621 is quite different from that of the posthumous edition of 1677 that had inspired Palombara.

According to a legend recorded in 1802 by the Italian bibliophile Francesco Girolamo Cancellieri, Marquis Palombara had lodged a passing Rosicrucian pilgrim, not recognised by non-believers, in his palace for the night. Some say that the pilgrim was the alchemist Francesco Giustiniani Bono, who gave his disciple a powder to manufacture gold together with a mysterious manuscript filled with esoteric symbols that contained the secret of the Philosopher's Stone. These symbols may well be those inscribed around the door, the threshold of which was incidentally crossed the next morning by the mysterious sage, who disappeared for ever.

VSTODIT DRACO ET
CVSTASSET IASON
DIAMETER SPHER
CRVX ORBIS
NON ORBIS PROSV

09.

Sant'Eusebio church
Piazza Vittorio Emanuele II, du côté de la via Napoleone III
Metro A – Vittorio Emanuele; Tram 5, 14 – Principe Eugenio/Manzoni

BLESSING OF THE ANIMALS AT SANT'EUSEBIO

Bless your pet, horse or cow...

Every year on 17 January, people have their animals blessed in front of this church. This used to happen in front of the church on Via Carlo Alberto dedicated to Saint Anthony the Abbot, protector of animals, but the function was transferred to the front of Sant'Eusebio church because of traffic problems.

Although today this centuries-old tradition only concerns pets, in the past it was a rite concerning all animals, including horses, cows and other farmyard animals. Farmers having their animals blessed had to bring an offering in kind to the church, whereas nobles were asked for money, donations of various other types and large candles which were said to protect the animals from all harm. In fact, the number of nobles asking for private services for their animals excessively increased the amount of money linked to the blessing, so other parishes tried to organise similar ceremonies in their churches.

The phenomenon grew to such an extent that it finally forced the cardinal vicar in 1831 to threaten to suspend a *divinis* any priests who carried out blessings on animals without permission.

10.

Piazza delle Repubblica
Metro A – Repubblica

THE SUNDIAL OF SANTA MARIA DEGLI ANGELI CHURCH

A testimonial to momentous reform

The Basilica of Santa Maria degli Angeli (Our Lady of the Angels) is a majestic basilica built within the Baths of Diocletian according to designs by Michelangelo, with later additions by Vanvitelli.

On the floor of the basilica in front of Diaz's tomb, one can admire a very beautiful sundial measuring 45 metres long, also called the *Linea Clementina* (Clementine Line) since it was inaugurated by Pope Clement XI on 6 October 1702.

This beautiful bronze and marble inlay had become rather worn after centuries of being trodden upon by churchgoers, but restoration work in 2000 rendered it in all its former beauty.

Its creation dates back to 1700, when, in order to check the accuracy of the Gregorian reform of the calendar, Pope Clement XI asked the mathematician and astronomer Francesco Bianchini to build a monumental sundial that would indicate the spring equinox and therefore help to determine the exact date of Easter Sunday.

According to the rules set out by the Fathers of the Church at the Council of Nicaea in 325, Easter was to be celebrated on the first Sunday after the first full moon following the spring equinox. Therefore it was extremely important to avoid mistakes that would have inevitably moved the dates of all the other movable religious holidays.

Alongside the sundial is another old marble inlay representing the signs of the Zodiac. These were based on Maratta's drawings, using the images of Bayer's *Uranometria Nova*.

To the right of the line, the signs of the summer and autumn constellations appear; to the left, those of spring and winter. Every day of the year at midday, the rays of the sun, entering the building through the centre of the heraldic coat of arms of Pope Clement XI, touch a different point of the line, advancing from Cancer during the summer solstice to Capricorn during the winter solstice, and then back through the rest of the signs to Cancer.

TERMINVS
PASCHAE
88
89
42 90
91
ORIONIS BALTHEI PRIMA
79° 11' 57"
92
93
43
94
ORIONIS BALTHEI MEDIA
80° 16' 6"
95
ORIONIS BALTHEI VLTIMA
81° 25' 46"
96
LIBRAE LANX BOREALIS
44
225° 15' 7"
97

HOW DOES A MERIDIAN WORK?

Instead of using the shadow of a gnomon, meridians use a small hole placed at a certain height, through which the sun's light falls onto a meridian line (i.e. one aligned exactly north–south). The fact that the sun's rays perform the function of the shadow in a traditional sundial means that the opening is sometimes referred to as a 'gnomonic opening'.

The higher the opening, the more efficient the meridian, hence the interest in using cathedrals; the circumference of the hole had to be no more than one thousandth of the height above the ground. Obviously, the opening had to be installed on the south side of the building in order to let in the rays of the sun, which lies to the south in the northern hemisphere.

The meridian line should run from the point which stands perpendicularly below the axis of the opening, not always easy to determine using the instruments available to scientists in the past.

The length of the line depends on the height of the opening; in some cases, where the building was not long enough to trace the entire meridian line across the floor (as was the case at Saint-Sulpice in Paris), an obelisk was added at its end, so that the movement of the sun's rays could then be measured up the vertical. In summer, when the sun is highest in the sky, the sun's rays fall onto the meridian line closer to the south wall (where that line begins) than they do in winter, when the sun is lower over the horizon and the rays tend to strike towards the far end of the meridian line.

The main principle behind the working of the meridian is that at noon, solar time, the sun is at its apex and, by definition, its rays fall straight along a line running exactly north–south. So, the exact moment when those rays strike the meridian line, which does run north–south, indicates the solar noon.

Furthermore, the exact place on the meridian line where the rays fall makes it possible to determine the day of the year: the point right at the beginning of the line is reached solely on the day of the summer solstice, while the exact end of the line is reached on the day of the winter solstice.

Experience and observation meant that the meridian line could be calibrated to identify different days of the year.

Once this was done, the line could be used to establish the date of various movable feasts, such as Easter – one of the great scientific and religious uses of meridians.

Similarly, the different periods corresponding with the signs of the Zodiac could be established, which explains why such signs are indicated along the length of a number of meridian lines.

The word 'leap year' owes its name to the fact that the extra day was inserted between 24 and 25 February. According to the Latin name, 24 February was the sixth (sextus) day before the calends of March, hence the term bis sextus for the extra day. The calends were the first day of each month in the Roman calendar.

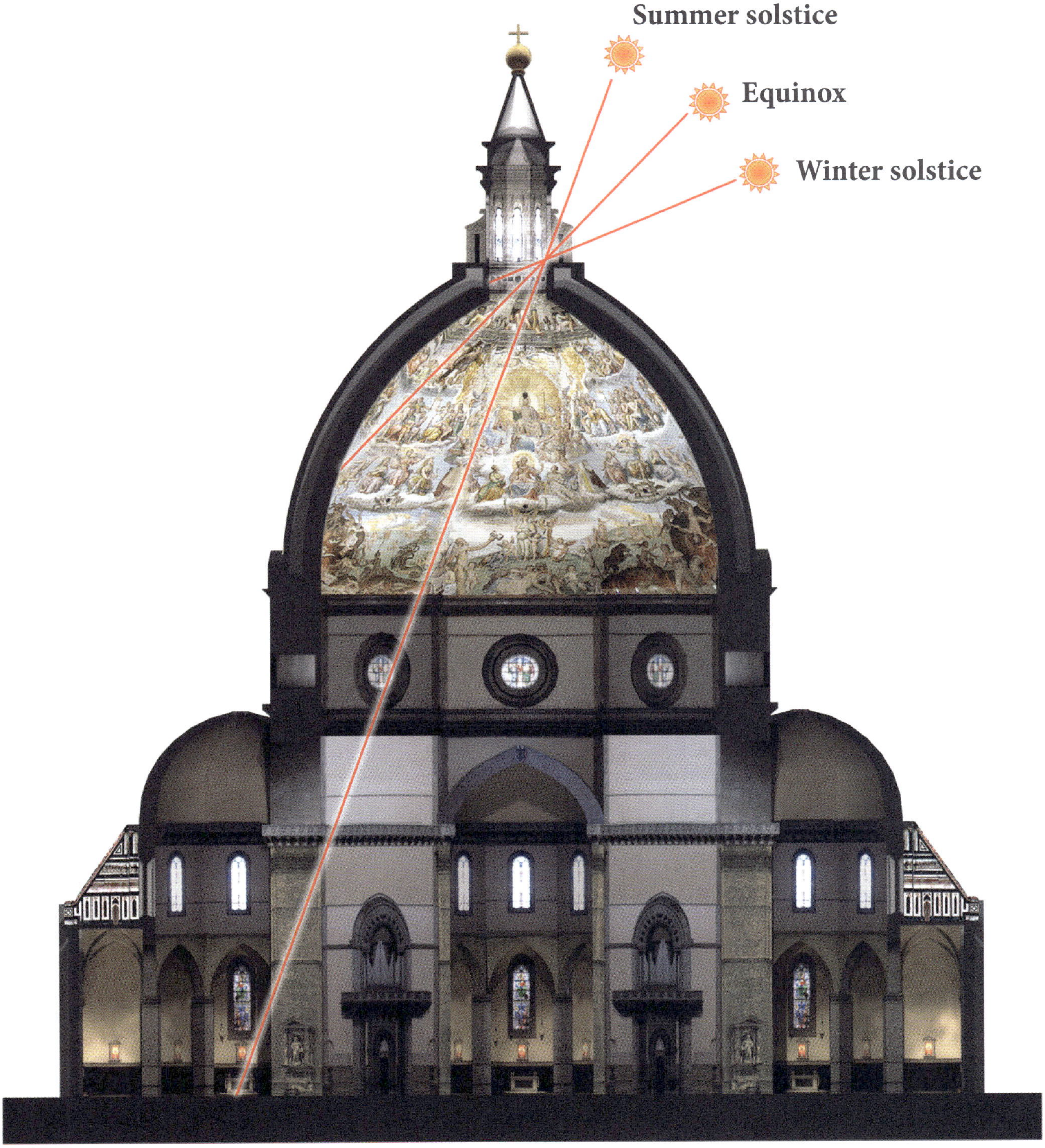
Summer solstice
Equinox
Winter solstice

11.

Piazza della Repubblica
Metro A – Repubblica

THE BOREAL MERIDIAN OF SANTA MARIA DEGLI ANGELI CHURCH

The only meridian in the world for tracking the pole star

Although the solar meridian of Santa Maria degli Angeli is relatively well known, the extraordinary boreal meridian also found in the transept of this church is much less so. Oriented north, in contrast to the sundial which is oriented south, this boreal meridian is the only known example of its kind.

It is intended to track on the church floor the movement around the North Pole of the pole star (Polaris), which can be seen through a hole located high up (27.20 m) on the right wing of the church. Near the beginning of the solar meridian, 17 magnificent ellipses correspond to the various trajectories of the star. This boreal meridian is an extraordinary and rare instrument that makes it possible to measure the effect of the precession of the equinoxes.

Aside from its astronomical function, Bianchini's meridian also marks the midnight hour, corresponding to the beginning of the ecclesiastical day (see also preceding double-page spread).

Further detail on the operation of the two meridians of Santa Maria degli Angeli church can be found in the remarkable book *Il cielo in Basilica* (Italian only, Agami publishers).

WHERE DOES THE WORD 'BOREAL' COME FROM?

In Greek mythology, Boreas was the son of Eos and Astraeus and personified the north wind. The adjective boreal, by extension, denotes the north or northern regions.

STELLAE POLARIS ORBITA
21
22
23

It was September 1995 and Thomas Jonglez was in Peshawar, the northern Pakistani city, 20 kilometres from the tribal zone he was to visit a few days later. It occurred to him that he should record the hidden aspects of his native city, Paris, which he knew so well. During his seven-month trip back home from Beijing, the countries he crossed included Iran and Kurdistan. He never took a plane but travelled by boat, train or bus, hitchhiking, cycling, on horseback or on foot, reaching Paris just in time to celebrate Christmas with the family.

On his return, he spent two fantastic years wandering the streets of the capital to gather material for his first "secret guide", written with a friend. For the next seven years he worked in the steel industry until the passion for discovery overtook him. He launched Jonglez Publishing in 2003 and moved to Venice three years later.

In 2013, in search of new adventures, the family left Venice and spent six months travelling to Brazil, via North Korea, Micronesia, the Solomon Islands, Easter Island, Peru and Bolivia.

After seven years in Rio de Janeiro, he now lives in Berlin with his wife and three children.

Jonglez Publishing produces a range of titles in nine languages, released in 40 countries.

Atlas of curiosities

Atlas of abandoned France
Atlas of extreme weather
Atlas of forbidden places
Atlas of geographical curiosities
Atlas of geographical curiosities - Britain
Atlas of unusual wines
Atlas of urban vineyards

Secret Atlas

Berlin - The secret atlas
London - The secret atlas
New York - The secret atlas
Paris - The secret atlas
Venice - The secret atlas

'Soul of' guides

Soul of Amsterdam
Soul of Athens
Soul of Barcelona
Soul of Berlin
Soul of Brussels
Soul of Detroit
Soul of Kyoto
Soul of Lisbon
Soul of Los Angeles
Soul of Marrakesh
Soul of Marseille
Soul of Milan
Soul of New York
Soul of Paris
Soul of Rome
Soul of Tokyo
Soul of Venice
Soul of Vienna

Photo books

Abandoned America
Abandoned Asylums
Abandoned Australia
Abandoned Belgium
Abandoned Churches: Unclaimed places of worship
Abandoned cinemas of the world
Abandoned France
Abandoned Germany
Abandoned Italy
Abandoned Japan
Abandoned Lebanon
Abandoned Spain
Abandoned USSR
Abandoned world – An AI-generated exploration
After the Final Curtain – The Fall of the American Movie Theater
After the Final Curtain – America's Abandoned Theaters
Baikonur – Vestiges of the Soviet space programme
Cinemas – A French heritage
Clickbait – A visual journey through AI-generated stories
Forbidden France
Forbidden Places – Vol. 1
Forbidden Places – Vol. 2
Forbidden Places – Vol. 3
Forgotten France
Forgotten Heritage
Oblivion
Parisian Theatres
Secret sacred sites
Venice deserted
Venice from the skies

'Secret' guides

Secret Amsterdam
Secret Bali – An unusual guide
Secret Bangkok
Secret Barcelona
Secret Bath – An unusual guide
Secret Belfast
Secret Berlin
Secret Boston – An unusual guide
Secret Brighton – An unusual guide
Secret Brooklyn – An unusual guide
Secret Brussels
Secret Budapest
Secret Buenos Aires
Secret Campania
Secret Cape Town
Secret Copenhagen
Secret Corsica
Secret Dolomites
Secret Dublin – An unusual guide
Secret Edinburgh – An unusual guide
Secret Florence
Secret French Riviera
Secret Geneva
Secret Glasgow
Secret Granada
Secret Helsinki
Secret Istanbul
Secret Johannesburg
Secret Kuala Lumpur
Secret Lisbon
Secret Liverpool – An unusual guide
Secret London – An unusual guide
Secret London – Unusual bars & restaurants
Secret Los Angeles – An unusual guide
Secret Louisiana – An unusual guide
Secret Madrid
Secret Mexico City
Secret Milan
Secret Montreal – An unusual guide
Secret Naples
Secret New Orleans – An unusual guide
Secret New York – An unusual guide
Secret New York – Curious activities
Secret New York – Hidden bars & restaurants
Secret Normandy
Secret Paris
Secret Potsdam
Secret Prague
Secret Provence
Secret Rio de Janeiro
Secret Rome
Secret Seville
Secret Singapore
Secret Stockholm
Secret Strasbourg
Secret Sussex – An unusual guide
Secret Tokyo
Secret Tuscany
Secret Venice
Secret Venice Lagoon
Secret Vienna
Secret Washington D.C. – An unusual guide
Secret York – An unusual guide

Follow us on Facebook and Instagram

CREDITS

Adriano Morabito (texts and photos): Hand on Via dei Cerchi, Pope's railway, Rooms of Saint Aloysius de Gonzaga, Bas-relief depicting the Judgement of Pâris, White marble discs of St Peter's Square, Bust of Father Secchi, Miraculous waters of the Madonna del Pozzo, Hypogeum cemetery of Santa Maria dell'Orazione e Morte Church, Old pharmacy of Santa Maria della Scala, *Titulus equitii* below the basilica of San Martino ai Monti (p. 281), National Museum of the History of Medicine.

Alessandra Zucconi: Miraculous waters of the Madonna del Pozzo, Private tour of Palazzo Sacchetti, The cover of the 'Terrina' fountain, Istituto nazionale di Studi Romani.

Brasil embassy: Palazzo Pamphilj.

Assaf Shoshan: Roman cistern at Villa Medici.

Beatrice Pediconi: Private tour of Palazzo Sacchetti (photo).

Damiano Vergari: Façade of Palazzo Zuccari (photo left page), Sanctuary of our lady of the small arch (photo right page), Cat of Palazzo Grazioli (text and photo), Marble foot (text and photo), Nerone's heart of stone (text and photo), Saw of the Church of Santa Maria in Monserrato degli Spagnoli (text and photo), Bust of Negrita (text and photo), Square halo of Santa Prassede Basilica (photo right page), Marquis Palombara's Porta Alchemica (photo page 241).

DR: Boreal meridian of Santa Maria degli Angeli church, Sundial of Santa Maria degli Angeli church.

Galzu: Symbolism of the Fontanella delle Tre Tiare.

Ginevra Lovatelli: Cannon ball of Viale della Trinità dei Monti fountain, Façade of Palazzo Zuccari (left page), Hendrik Christian Andersen Museum, Monumental hall of the Vallicelliana Library, Monte di Piétà Chapel, Cappella Spada, Biblioteca Casanatense, The boarded-up window at Palazzo Mattei, Monumental complex of Santo Spirito in Sassia, The Italian clock of the Palazzo del Commendatore, The foundlings' wheel, Saint Peter's meridian, San Pietro in Montorio's cannon ball, Cloisters of the Nuovo Regina Margherita Hospital, Old pharmacy of Santa Maria della Scala, Orange tree of Santa Sabina cloister, The hiding place of Saint Alexius, Table of Santa Barbara Oratory, Musei di Patologia del libro, Blessing of the animals at Sant'Eusebio, Cannon ball in the Aurelian wall, Princess Isabelle's apartment.

Hélène Vuillermet (texts and photos): Anatomy theatre of San Gallicano Hospital, National Museum of the History of Medicine.

Jacopo Barbarigo: Poussin's tomb, Secret rooms of Saint Philip Neri, Mass in Aramaic at Santa Maria Church in Campo Marzio, Stag of Sant'Eustachio church, Figures missing from the Arch of the Moneychangers, Triple enclosures of San Giovanni in Laterano cloister, Verbal abuse in Basilica San Clemente, Statue of Stanislas Kostka.

Jebulon: Hidden symbolism of Bernini's elephant-obelisk.

Koen Ivens: Baker's tomb.

Marco Gradozzi (texts and photos): Villa Maraini, Tour of the Angelica Library, Scar on a marble column (photo right page), Sanctuary of our lady of the small arch, Outline of the former ghetto fountain, American Academy in Rome, Gardens of the Knights of Malta priory, Game in the cloister of Santi Quattro Coronati Basilica, X-rated frescoes in St Stephen's.

Mikhail Malykh: Marquis Palombara's Porta Alchemica (photo page 239).

Florence Museum of the History of Science: How does a meridian work?

Ophilia Ramnauth: Galileo's column (text and photos), Roman cistern at Villa Medici (text).

Peter1936F: Cardinal Bessarion's chapel.

Sailko: Plaque designating the original location of the obelisk on St. Peter's Square.

Valerio Ceva Grimaldi: Façade of Palazzo Zuccari (photo right page), Old pharmacy of Santa Maria della Scala (photo left page).

Cover photo: © Spencer Davis - Unsplash

Maps: **Cyrille Suss** – Layout: **Emmanuelle Willard Toulemonde** –
Translation: **Caroline Lawrence, Jana Gough, Ordentop and Olivia Fuller** – English editing: **Sigrid Newman** –
Proofreading: **Dikshit Akbari** – Publishing: **Clémence Mathé**

Edition: 01
ISBN: 978-2-36195-970-8
Printed in China by Toppan – October 2026

MIX
Paper | Supporting responsible forestry
FSC® C104723